AMERICAN DREAM

Charles Ancelle

www.dizzyemupublishing.com

DIZZY EMU PUBLISHING

1714 N McCadden Place, Hollywood, Los Angeles 90028

www.dizzyemupublishing.com

American Dream

Charles Ancelle

ISBN-13: 978-1537531465

First published in the United States

in 2016 by Dizzy Emu Publishing

www.dizzyemupublishing.com

AMERICAN DREAM

Written by

Charles Ancelle

Draft 4.0

c.ancelle@hotmail.fr
(347) 331-4118

EXT. ROAD - NIGHT

The middle of the night. Crickets fill the air with their
musical beats, otherwise, all is dead.

A bassy car engine RUMBLES and approaches.

The silhouette of an old sedan appears in the horizon, it
moves suspiciously slow with its beams turned off.

INT. SEDAN - NIGHT

Two GIRLS sit quietly at the front.

The driver,

SASHA (22), beautiful but tough, with the expression of
someone who's struggled her whole life, drives while,

DARIA (16), her younger sister, eager to prove herself,
thinks she knows more than she does,

Sits next to her.

The car comes to a stop.

> SASHA
> (in Russian)
> Stay here.

> DARIA
> (also in Russian)
> Why?

> SASHA
> You need to watch the car.

> DARIA
> I wanna come with you.

> SASHA
> That's not a discussion. Keep your
> ass here.

She pulls out a tiny PISTOL from the glove compartment and
puts it in her pants. She opens her door.

EXT. SEDAN - NIGHT

Everything around her is so dark it's hard to get a sense of
where she is, but Sasha walks around to the trunk and pulls
out a headlight, which she puts on, and a pair of PLIERS.

She flips around the car and reaches the passenger window, which Daria rolls down.

> SASHA
> I'll be back in two hours at most.
> If not, leave.

> DARIA
> You better come back. We're way too
> close.

The shadow of a smile on Sasha's face before the two girls give each other a brief hug.

EXT. FOREST - NIGHT

Sasha walks cautiously through uninviting woods, now intermittently lit from her dim headlight.

She keeps looking around, as if expecting to get caught any moment, and continues quietly.

Suddenly, a DROP of rain falls onto her. Then another, until suddenly a heavy rain starts to DRENCH HER completely.

> SASHA
> (to herself in Russian)
> Fuck me.

She begins to move a lot faster.

EXT. BORDER - NIGHT

BARBED WIRES enclose a TRENCH, six to seven feet deep and wide.

It's still incredibly dark, Sasha has turned off her headlight. She approaches the wires, looks around one more time, then places the PLIERS on a wire at her eye level.

CHUNK. One done, many more to go.

CHUNK. One more. She clearly isn't doing this for the first time.

MOMENTS LATER

Sasha cuts the last wire she needs in order to get through.

She goes through the hole just cut, and SLIDES down the TRENCH.

Looks around, takes a deep breath.

A BORDER PATROL CAR passes through the road right next to
her. She quickly goes to hide against the trench.

The car doesn't stop. She gets up, and CLIMBS up the trench
with the PLIERS.

She reaches the second row of barbed wires, and begins to
cut.

EXT. FARM - NIGHT

Sasha walks cautiously through a field of mud.

She stops, she can see a car parked in the middle of nowhere
with its lights shining in the horizon.

MOMENTS LATER

She reaches the car, now visibly surrounded by four ARMED
MEN.

The TALLEST one takes a step forward, his RIFLE pointed at
Sasha, followed by a LANKY MAN, holding an umbrella for him.

>   TALL MAN
>   (in Russian)
>   We've got to have forbidden fruit.

>   SASHA
>   (also in Russian)
>   Or Eden's joys for us are moot.

>   TALL MAN
>   (to Sasha)
>   No issue?

>   SASHA
>   None.

He points his flashlight at her to check if she's lying. This
is the first time we fully see her face. If she's lying, it's
impossible to tell.

He nods, lowers his rifle, and gives her an attaché-case. She
grabs it, and waits as the tall man lights a cigarette.

>   SASHA (CONT'D)
>   Can I have that umbrella?

>   TALL MAN
>   Why do you need an umbrella?

                         SASHA
               So I can count?

                         TALL MAN
               You don't need an umbrella to
               count.

                         SASHA
               No, I need one to keep the dough
               dry.

They eye duel for a bit. The tall man takes a drag and smiles
at her. He makes a sign to the lanky man, who walks over to
Sasha and holds the umbrella above her.

She opens the attaché-case and begins to count the many 500
euro bills stacked inside.

EXT. BORDER - NIGHT

Sasha, now going back the other way with her case in hand,
approaches the barbed wires she cut off earlier.

Thick drops of rain continue to shower her more than ever.

She stops, takes a careful look on both sides of the adjacent
road, then crosses it to reach the barbed wires.

She throws the case through the hole first, then slips her
leg in, then her upper body, to finish with her other leg
which gets STUCK against the wire.

She tries to pull it, which leads her to CUT herself, she
GROANS in pain before she hears an ENGINE ROAR nearby. She
turns around and sees dim LIGHTS in the distance.

She takes a deep breath and tries to pull the stuck wire out,
but to no avail.

The engine gets closer, the beams brighter.

Now she pulls back using all her body weight but her other
leg begins to SINK into the mud with the effort.

The car is now almost there, she has maybe a few seconds left
before she gets caught.

Sasha THROWS all the strength she has, and finally, her leg
comes free, and she flies backwards into the trench with the
case still in her hand.

She looks up as what is now clearly a PATROL CAR stops right
next to her hole.

She looks around, panicked, then crawls several feet away from where she fell, and begins to roll herself in the WET MUD.

She hears the car's door open. Footsteps. A flashlight illuminates the side of the trench facing her.

But the rain clutters visibility.

> VOICE
> (in Russian)
> What the fuck are you doing?

Sasha continues to cover herself with mud.

> DEEPER VOICE
> (in Russian)
> Thought I saw something.

> VOICE
> Like what?

She now starts to bury the case in the mud with herself.

> DEEPER VOICE
> Look.

Closer footsteps. Eerie silence.

The flashlight beam stops in one spot, then illuminates the first hole Sasha cut on the other side.

Sasha's chest begins to contract at a fast pace.

The sounds of someone going through the wires. Then quiet--

The flashlight beam now moves along the bottom of the trench, goes over Sasha.

> VOICE
> See anything?

The beam stops near her. She holds her breath.

> DEEPER VOICE
> No.

Without rain, the guard would spot her, but her camouflage works here.

The beam goes away and moves to the barbed wires on the other side. Silence.

.

RATATATATA! Bullets WHIZ all over the wires.

She coils herself as tight as possible, and shivers.

> VOICE
> They're probably gone.

> DEEPER VOICE
> Just in case.

More footsteps. Two doors opening and closing. The engine starts again, roars, and off the car goes.

Sasha continues to breathe in fear, frozen, until she decides to get up.

She picks up the case to lift it from the mud, and pulls it up with herself.

She reaches the top, and hurries through the hole she initially cut.

I/E. SEDAN - NIGHT

Daria sleeps against the window as drops of rain continue to shower it on the outside.

She snores gently until--

BANG!

She JUMPS up from her seat as Sasha appears against the door making a zombie face which, with all the mud covering her, is pretty effective.

Daria unlocks the car and rolls her window down.

> SASHA
> Can you look after the case for a minute? Gotta go take a piss.

> DARIA
> In the rain?

> SASHA
> Want me to do it in the car?

> DARIA
> I could use a shower.

The two of them grin at each other. Sasha hands her the case and walks off.

Daria brushes mud off the case and examines it with a mixture of fear and reverence.

She looks around. Sasha seems far, definitely can't see her.

She opens the case, looks inside, and for a fleeting moment, her eyes fill up with greed.

She looks around one more time, looks back, picks up a few stacks of cash, counts the amount of bills, and takes out a bill from one, and from another, and another.

She looks around again. She pulls out a few more, then puts the stacks back in a hurry, closes the case, and shoves the bills she just took inside her pants.

Sasha appears on the other side of the car, opens the door, and gets in the driver's seat.

Daria looks at her innocently.

> DARIA (CONT'D)
> Did you touch yourself back there?

> SASHA
> Someone needs to get laid.

> DARIA
> *Someone* does.

Sasha smiles and starts the engine.

> SASHA
> When we get there, we'll both get
> laid.

EXT. ABANDONED FACTORY - NIGHT

Sasha's car, still no beams on, pulls up next to ruins of concrete and chimneys.

Sasha and Daria get out of the car, Sasha holding the case, and they walk through a wall's hole.

INT. ABANDONED FACTORY - NIGHT

Four UKRAINIAN CRIMINALS stand next to a small work light in the middle of the room, all armed.

None of them make a move. DMITRI (37), their leader, a skinhead that would scare off anyone with brains, turns to Daria.

                    DMITRI
               (in Russian)
          Who is she?

                    SASHA
          My sister.

                    DMITRI
          Why?

                    SASHA
          Training her.

Dmitri gets up and approaches Daria, ready to bite if needed.
Daria stays put.

He makes a sign to one of his guys, a STOUT MAN, who grabs
the case and opens it.

He begins to count the money. Daria watches him, we can sense
the horror inside of her, but she does a really good job
hiding it to everyone else.

                    DMITRI
          How'd she do?

                    SASHA
          Good.

The man finishes counting. Dmitri interrogates him with a
look, the man shakes his head.

Dmitri looks back at Sasha and Daria.

                    DMITRI
          My man tells me money is missing.

                    SASHA
          Shouldn't be, I counted myself, it
          was all there.

                    DMITRI
          Perhaps, you don't know how to
          count?

Sasha stays unphased.

                    SASHA
          No. It's all there.

                    DMITRI
          Count again.

The stout man begins to count again.

While he does so, Dmitri eyes Daria, who suddenly seems to be losing her cool.

> DMITRI (CONT'D)
> What's up darling?

> SASHA
> You intimidate her.

> DMITRI
> She can speak for herself.

> DARIA
> No-- Nothing.

Dmitri gets right in her face, his eyes right against hers, he reads her.

> DMITRI
> I think your little sister may be
> the reason for our disagreement.
> Hand it over.

> DARIA
> Wh-- What?

> DMITRI
> Play dumb one more time, and I will
> break your knees.

> DARIA
> I don't know-- what you-- talking
> about.

Sasha looks at her sister, dumbstruck.

> SASHA
> Come on, the cash is all there, I
> checked.

Dmitri gives her his hand to talk to, turns to Daria.

> DMITRI
> The cash. Now.

Daria looks at Sasha, her eyes tearing up.

Dmitri sighs and makes a sign.

A BUFF MAN points his rifle at Sasha while a SKINNY MAN walks over to Daria, and starts searching her.

He stops at her crotch, feels something there.

Sasha gets ready to jump but stops when she hears the rifle's safety click.

                    SASHA
          What the fuck do you think you're
          doing?

The skinny man tries to put his hand inside her pants but Daria KICKS him in the gut with her knee before he gets a chance.

The skinny man retaliates with a violent PUNCH in her face which leads her to fall down.

He then TACKLES her and puts his knee on her neck to block her movements as he proceeds to search her crotch--

And pulls out a small stack of 500 euro bills.

Dmitri turns to Sasha, raising his rifle.

                    DMITRI
          Interesting turn of event.

                    DARIA
          Please, Sasha didn't know, it's my
          fault.

Dmitri turns to Daria.

BAM! BAM! A bullet in each of her legs. She SCREAMS her lungs out and falls flat to the ground.

Sasha ROARS with rage as she tries to JUMP to Dmitri, but the other three guys grab her and KICK her repeatedly until she stops fighting.

Dmitri then kneels down next to Sasha, who is now on the ground, tears of rage mixing with her blood.

He takes the time to light a cigarette, thinking, then blows a bunch of smoke on her face.

                    DMITRI
          I don't get it. You girls just had
          to wait for a few more jobs. Your
          little American dream was waiting
          for you.

                    SASHA
          She didn't know what she was--

                    DMITRI
          She knew, and I think there is a
          chance you did too.

                    SASHA
          I swear Dmitri, I didn't, and she's
          still a child, I'll do anything I
          swear.

                    DMITRI
          You certainly will.

Sasha and Daria exchange painful, remorseful looks.

INT. COMMERCIAL AIRPLANE - DAY

The usual boarding commotion.

PASSENGERS push each other in their inexorable anxiety to
immediately get packed like a sardine for the next thirteen
hours.

Among them, Sasha OPENS the various compartments around her:
they're all full.

She carries a large SPORTS BAG and a backpack.

Unphased, she pushes one of the suitcases to the side as hard
as she can and slides her sports bag in.

She puts old headphones on, and sits in her window seat with
her backpack on her lap.

As she turns her music on, suddenly all the commotion around
her seems to disappear.

                    STEWARDESS (O.S.)
          Ladies & Gentlemen, welcome on
          board this Ukraine International
          Airlines flight two thirty six for
          New York JFK international Airport.
          We are ready for take off, please
          make sure your seat belts are
          fastened --

As she looks through the window, a tear rolls down her cheek,
unannounced.

EXT. JFK AIRPORT - DAWN

A 747 lowers its altitude and eclipses the rising sun.

INT. COMMERCIAL AIRPLANE - DAWN

Among the commotion, Sasha lets her NEIGHBOR (42) pick up the suitcases that were filling the compartment.

When he knocks her bag down with his, she CATCHES it with abnormal speed and nearly knocks him by doing so.

> NEIGHBOR
> Gee-- That was fast! You got drugs
> in there?

He sniggers at his own joke, she smiles back as much as she can.

INT. JET BRIDGE - DAWN

Sasha walks through the exit door with her eyes focused forward, but a few steps into the bridge, she stops to look through the window: this is her first real peak at America.

From this perspective, it looks strangely identical to the airport she left, but it's bigger of course, and there's an American Flag somewhere.

Other passengers walk past her, which she realizes quickly and decides to keep moving at a fast pace.

INT. CUSTOMS LINES - MOMENTS LATER

One one side, the free-flowing, almost empty U.S. Residents line.

On the other, the NON U.S. Residents line:

Hundreds of people, standing with their red tired eyes, leaning on whatever they can, eerily silent.

Among them, Sasha stands, slightly anxious, she looks around, it's clearly her first time.

INT. CUSTOMS BOOTH - MOMENTS LATER

Sasha stands at the edge of the line, waiting for her name to be called. Her fingers twitch a little.

At the booth, a middle-aged CUSTOMS OFFICER waves at her.

> CUSTOMS OFFICER
> Next!

Sasha calmly walks towards the officer, stops in front, and gives her passport.

                    SASHA
          Hi.

The officer ignores her, takes the passport and examines it.

                    CUSTOMS OFFICER
          Flying in from Ukraine?

                    SASHA
          Yes.

                    CUSTOMS OFFICER
          Reason for your visit?

                    SASHA
          Tourism.

                    CUSTOMS OFFICER
          You're visiting by yourself?

                    SASHA
          Yes.

                    CUSTOMS OFFICER
          Where are you staying?

Sasha hands him a piece of paper.

                    SASHA
          This address.

                    CUSTOMS OFFICER
          Where is that?

                    SASHA
          Brooklyn.

                    CUSTOMS OFFICER
          For how long you gonna be there?

                    SASHA
          One week.

                    CUSTOMS OFFICER
          Can I see your return tickets?

Sasha nods. She flips through her backpack, looking for her ticket. The officer takes a peak inside the backpack as well.

She takes out the ticket. The officer takes a look at it for an unnecessarily long period of time. Then stares at Sasha, looking for a crack.

She stares back at him, confident, she knows she'll be okay as long as everything seems normal.

                    CUSTOMS OFFICER (CONT'D)
          Place your left thumb on the screen
          please.

INT. LUGGAGE INSPECTION BAY - DAY

Sasha's sports bag dangles against her hip and her backpack as she moves swiftly towards a luggage inspection OFFICER, her passport and entry form in hand.

A few TRAVELERS wait in line ahead of her, and pass without question.

A subtle trickle of sweat appears on her forehead as she patiently waits a few feet away for the next traveler to move forward.

The officer finally makes a sign to her to approach, which she does immediately.

He eyes her with suspicion, like the customs officer.

                    OFFICER
          What's in the sports bag?

                    SASHA
          Just clothes.

He watches her for a few seconds, she gazes around the room, suddenly curious of her surroundings, worry-free.

                    OFFICER
          Next!

INT. JFK AIRPORT - ARRIVALS - MOMENTS LATER

Sasha walks among the confused horde of tired passengers with a steady pace, nearing the finish line of the marathon to get out of there.

A never ending line of people seems to almost block access to the exit, all anxiously waiting for their loved ones.

Sasha scans the line, it seems like someone should be waiting for her there, but she can't see him.

She reaches a spot where she can stop and look around.

                    VICTOR (O.S.)
          Sasha?

She startles and turns around to face **VICTOR SHEVCHENKO** (42),
charismatic, soft-spoken, average looking aside from a goatee
that could make Jafar envious, and a small neck tatoo.

He approaches Sasha with a benevolent smile.

                    SASHA
          He broke my heart.

                    VICTOR
          You merely broke my life.

*NOTE: Sasha speaks English with a strong Ukrainian accent.
Victor speaks English with the accent of someone who moved to
the US when he was in his teens.*

                    VICTOR (CONT'D)
          Welcome to America. Let me carry
          the bag for you.

He takes it from her, she watches him defiantly but doesn't
try to stop him.

                    VICTOR (CONT'D)
          All right, let's go to my car.

INT. JFK PARKING LOT - DAY

Victor and Sasha, now by themselves aside from a few other
travelers in the background, walk along a long line of cars
when Victor unlocks a nearby GRAY CIVIC.

He pops the trunk open and puts the bag in it.

                    SASHA
          You not going to check it?

                    VICTOR
          Not here.

                    SASHA
          Where?

                    VICTOR
          You'll see.

He opens the passenger door and gives her a sign to come in.
She gives him a hesitant look.

                         VICTOR (CONT'D)
          Hop in.

She hesitates a little more, then decides to get in.

INT. CIVIC - DAY

Victor and Sasha sit quietly as they stand in traffic on
fifth avenue and central park south. Passersby move fluidly
around them.

Sasha looks out the window, doing her best to hide her
amazement.

                         VICTOR
               There's nothing quite like it, huh?

                         SASHA
          No.

                         VICTOR
               Our mutual friend tells me you'd
               like to move here someday?

                         SASHA
               I don't think I can do that, now.

                         VICTOR
               Because of your sister?

                         SASHA
               Why you asking questions if you
               already know everything?

Victor smirks.

                         VICTOR
               Just making conversation. We can
               talk about the weather if you
               prefer?

                         SASHA
               Or we can say nothing.

Victor smirks some more.

                         VICTOR
               I don't like bullshit either.
               Sounds good.

He turns up the music in the car.

INT. CIVIC - MOMENTS LATER

The sound of an engine slowing down.

Sasha slowly opens her eyes and realizes she just dozed off momentarily.

She looks out the window and sees they are now in some INDUSTRIAL area, parked in front of a dirty WAREHOUSE.

Victor turns off the engine.

                    SASHA
          How much did I sleep?

                    VICTOR
          Not long.

He smiles and opens the door.

EXT. WAREHOUSE - DAY

Victor opens the trunk, grabs the sports bag as Sasha gets out of the car and looks around the warehouse: it's eerily quiet.

Victor takes out a key and opens the door to the warehouse.

He holds the door for Sasha to enter.

                    VICTOR
          After you.

Sasha takes a peak through the door, but it's just darkness from there.

She nods and slowly walks into the warehouse. Victor closes the door after her.

INT. WAREHOUSE - CONTINUOUS

As the door closes, everything turns pitch black for a brief moment.

Sasha's echoing footsteps reveal the vast emptiness of the place.

CLICK. Victor turns the lights on and startles Sasha when he appears out of thin air right beside her.

He notices and chuckles.

> VICTOR
> I'm sorry, I didn't mean to startle
> you. This place is a little creepy.

He drops the sports bag on the floor.

> VICTOR (CONT'D)
> Shall we?

He points to the bag. Sasha looks down, then kneels down next to it.

She unzips the bag slowly and carefully, and finally opens it to reveal--

CLOTHES.

She removes a layer: more clothes.

As she begins to turn to Victor to see his reaction, a NEEDLE penetrates her neck, and Victor's hand injects her with a transparent liquid through it.

> VICTOR (CONT'D)
> You're the package this time,
> honey.

Sasha GRABS Victor's hand and starts to resist as she GASPS for air, but slowly, her grasp loosens, her eyelids lower, and her vision blurs.

> FADE TO BLACK.

INT. BLACK ROOM - NIGHT

Everything is a blur. Sasha's eyelids begin to blink, but even then, everything's dark, aside from a slit of light below the door.

Sasha begins to look around as her vision gets sharper.

> SASHA
> (in Russian)
> Hello?

She tries to move only to realize her entire body is TIED UP to a vertical pole.

> SASHA (CONT'D)
> Help! Anybody there?
> (switching to English)
> Help! Hello!

The door creaks open. One SILHOUETTE emerges from the threshold and walks to Sasha:

OSCAR (47), South-African, with the eerie smoothness of someone who could very well be a psychopath or simply in total control of any situation.

>   SASHA (CONT'D)
>   Hello? Who are you?

Oscar stops inches away from her, and suddenly SHINES a FLASHLIGHT right in her face.

She closes her eyes and tries her best to turn away, but he simply turns off the flash light and walks away.

>   SASHA (CONT'D)
>   What are you doing? Help me!

He closes the door behind him, but moments later, the door opens again, this time with the silhouettes of Victor, Oscar and

MEGAN (43), a madame with too much make up, old fashioned, and clearly having trouble ageing.

Victor turns on a dim bare light bulb hanging from the ceiling and approaches Sasha with a smile as Oscar remains in the back, watching from the shadows.

Sasha squirms like an enraged animal but with no success.

>   VICTOR
>   Hi!

He PUNCHES her in the gut like he would a punching bag. She GASPS for air as he pats his knuckle.

He then grabs her by the chin to make sure she looks at him.

He holds up her passport right in front of her face. Waits a few seconds to make sure she got it.

>   VICTOR (CONT'D)
>   Two things. One: I now own you.
>   Two: Your sister is dead.

A much deeper stab than any physical pain she's endured so far.

>   SASHA
>   I don't believe you.

Victor takes out his phone and shows it to Sasha.

ON PHONE SCREEN

A picture of Daria, bloody, on the floor, lifeless.

ON SASHA

Pure devastation. She can't quite comprehend, she freezes.

                    SASHA (CONT'D)
          That's impossible.

                    VICTOR
          If you don't want to end up like
          her, you'll do as we say. We clear?

He punches her in the gut again, then walks off as she
struggles to regain her breath.

Sasha begins to SQUIRM within her ties again. Megan takes a
step forward and starts to examine her, doctor-like, trying
to soothe her.

                    MEGAN
          Hush, hush.

Sasha watches her like a caged animal, ready to strike as she
continues to squirm.

Megan takes out a pair of sharp SCISSORS, which she slowly
runs along Sasha's cheek, to calm her down. It works. Sasha's
breathing decelerates.

                    MEGAN (CONT'D)
          If you calm down, I'll cut your
          ties. If you don't, I'll cut
          something else.

It works a little bit. Sasha's eyes remain full of rage, but
she allows Megan to begin cutting her ties.

                    MEGAN (CONT'D)
          Very good.

As Megan proceeds, Sasha calms down and begins to control
herself, almost eerily silent.

But as Megan cuts the last tie, Sasha swiftly GRABS Megan's
scissor-holding wrist, grabs the scissors with her other
hand, and motions to plant them into Megan's eyes, but--

Megan is able to stop Sasha's strike. The two of them arm-
wrestle with the scissors' edge millimeters from Megan's eye
when--

Oscar grabs Sasha's wrist, twists it like she were a child, inducing her to drop the scissors and kneel down immediately.

Megan quickly regains her breath, pulls out a TASER from her pocket, and TASES Sasha, who CONVULSES madly and DROPS to the floor.

Oscar grabs her gently and lifts her up, helping her lean against his shoulder.

Megan gets in her face, still flushed with anger at almost losing an eye. She SLAPS Sasha to help her regain consciousness.

Sasha slowly opens her eyes, dazed and confused.

                    MEGAN (CONT'D)
          Can you hear me?

Sasha clearly can as she fixes her hateful eyes on Megan.

                    MEGAN (CONT'D)
          Next time you do that, I'll take
          out *your* eye.

INT. BASEMENT CORRIDOR - MOMENTS LATER

Megan and Oscar lead Sasha through a dark, low-ceilinged, spiderwebbed corridor that feels more like a bunker's tunnel than anything else.

As they take a few quiet steps forward, they cross paths with two GIRLS walking in the opposite direction one after the other, who both avoid eye contact with Megan and give Sasha very brief looks.

They reach a door, which Megan opens. Oscar stays put.

INT. CHANGING ROOM - MOMENTS LATER

Megan leads Sasha inside this square, bare room decorated by several sets of shelves on each wall, each supporting piles of identical UNIFORMS.

In the middle, a square wooden bench hosts half a dozen GIRLS as they themselves change into the same uniform which appears to be a MAID OUTFIT.

Some finish putting tights on while others still button the upper part, but they all stop when they see Megan and Sasha enter.

> MEGAN
> Keep going, you all know what
> you're doing.

They all resume their activities.

Megan grabs a uniform from a shelf and throws it at Sasha.

> MEGAN (CONT'D)
> Put this on.

Sasha faces her, rebellious. Megan takes a step forward.

> MEGAN (CONT'D)
> Put. This. On.

Sasha takes a deep breath. She needs to tread carefully. She starts putting the outfit on.

> MEGAN (CONT'D)
> Faster.

Sasha doesn't really accelerate. Megan walks over to her and rips off her sweater.

> MEGAN (CONT'D)
> I said. Faster.

The other girls pretend not to see, except one:

ELENA (24), Colombian, who has something tender and motherly about her.

Sasha now finishes taking off her pants and begins to unfold the uniform Megan handed her.

INT. BASEMENT CORRIDOR - MOMENTS LATER

Megan and Oscar continue to lead Sasha through the same corridor.

On each side, Sasha notices barred doors giving access to small cells, *jail*.

Most of the cells are empty, some of them have some girls sitting or lying down idle inside, staring back at Sasha.

Sasha barely looks at her surroundings, she doesn't seem to understand yet that she is in a slave brothel.

She reaches down her butt and begins to scratch it when--

They reach a door at the end of the corridor, protected by
ROY (32), more of a pitbull than a man.

>   ROY
>   She the new one, huh?

He eyes Sasha with shameless lust.

>   MEGAN
>   Yeah, she's gonna settle in two-
>   thirty-seven.

Roy writes it down on a note pad, then moves to let them
through.

INT. STAIRCASE - CONTINUOUS

Megan, Oscar and Sasha continue up the staircase, each of
their thump echoing upward.

Sasha barely avoids stepping over a cockroach, almost loses
her balance, but Oscar catches her and pushes her to
continue.

They reach the first level door, protected by a large metal
LOCK.

They continue on to the next level, and finally reach the
fourth level, which is unprotected.

INT. FOURTH FLOOR CORRIDOR - CONTINUOUS

Megan and Oscar lead Sasha through what now appears to be a
hotel corridor. Doors with room numbers replace the dingy
cells from below.

They reach room number 234. Megan and Oscar stop in front of
it. She takes out a key, hands it to Sasha.

>   MEGAN
>   Open it.

Sasha takes the key, looks between Megan and Oscar, and RUNS
away from them as fast as she can.

It's not a rational, thought out run, it's a desperate move,
but she runs fast. Oscar and Megan struggle to keep up with
her.

She is able to turn around a corner, continue onto the next
corridor.

The footsteps behind are going farther from her, she might have a shot at outrunning them.

Ahead of her, the elevators, next to them, an emergency staircase.

She goes for it, Oscar and Megan still lagging behind.

She gets to the door, opens it, and comes face to face with--

PETE (29) a tall, pervy looking security guard, who SLAMS his baton against her chest. She FALLS instantly.

He FALLS down on her, puts his knee against her upper chest, blocking her completely. But she doesn't fight back.

Everything around her seems to blur. The tears of grief finally start pouring out. She's lost on both counts.

It's over.

Megan finally arrives and hovers over her.

> MEGAN (CONT'D)
> She needs some time in the black
> room.

INT. BLACK ROOM - NIGHT

Back in the room Sasha was locked in earlier, but now her arms and legs are both SHACKLED, she is locked in a standing position, helpless.

She keeps her head down, all desire for life seems gone from her.

The door opens, Oscar enters by himself and approaches her.

He puts his hand on her chin, she instantly looks away, avoiding any physical contact.

> OSCAR
> You need to get hydrated. Drink
> this.

He offers her a glass of water which he puts to her lips.

She barely reacts, so he starts inclining the glass of water so water pours down her lips, it works, her throat gulps down the little stream of water that gets in.

> OSCAR (CONT'D)
> Things are about to get rough.

He takes a deep breath, watches at her one more time, she returns his gaze briefly, then he opens the door and lets in

OFFICER DUSTIN WAYNE (45).

He's the kind of cop who would fit in very well at a KKK meeting, but no one would really suspect him of it.

Oscar leaves as Dustin enters the room.

Dustin takes his hat off, almost respectfully and places it on a HOOK protruding from the wall.

He approaches Sasha.

> DUSTIN
> Hey there, how you doin'?

Sasha watches him indifferently. He smiles as his BADGE glitters slightly in the dark.

> DUSTIN (CONT'D)
> I hear you've been a bad girl.

Dustin goes behind her and breathes in her ear.

She JERKS away from him instinctively.

He grabs her by the waist, to keep her in check.

> DUSTIN (CONT'D)
> You know what I do to bad girls?

Sasha ignores him.

He goes around and stands in front of her, a big smile on his face.

He unzips his pants, drawing out every moment as Sasha watches him, trying to stay in control.

His pants fall down.

> DUSTIN (CONT'D)
> Surprise!

She holds his gaze, doing her best not to look disgusted. Then, calmly:

> SASHA
> I have pity for you.

He approaches her. She keeps holding his gaze.

                         DUSTIN
              All right.

He gets within arm's length - then HITS her in the stomach
with his BATON. She can't breathe. Another HIT in her chest.

                         DUSTIN (CONT'D)
              Just so you don't get any ideas.

TEARS pour out of her eyes in spite of her efforts to keep
them in.

He goes behind her, SLIDES down her panties.

We hear the SOUND of his condom wrapping around, and he
enters her.

She MOANS with a mixture of desperation and pure rage.

He puts his hand over her mouth. She BITES it as hard as she
can.

He keeps it there and smiles as BLOOD drips down his hand.

He gets more intense. SHE SQUIRMS as much as she can. The
SHACKLES ring with discordant tones.

RING.

RING.

RING.

Until he climaxes. His breathing slows down.

Her face now dripping with tears and snot, she lets go of his
hand, beaten.

He takes off his condom, and throws it by her feet.

She catches her breath as best she can, paralyzed.

He puts his pants back on. His hat back on. Draws it out
again, you can tell he's enjoying this just as much as the
rape itself.

Sasha COUGHS her lungs out.

He turns to her, puts his bleeding hand on her cheek.

                         DUSTIN (CONT'D)
              I'll see you soon, gorgeous. Say hi
              to the others for me.

He wipes the blood on her cheek, and leaves the room.

She looks on, staying strong until the door SLAMS behind him.

Now she just CRUMBLES on herself and lets the rest of the tears come through.

MOMENTS LATER

There is no sense of time in that room, but we can see by the state of Sasha's bruises that some time has passed.

Several condoms on the floor: other men have come here as well.

When the door opens, she doesn't look up, she looks entirely broken.

Oscar takes a few steps toward her.

She continues to look down.

He wraps a warm BLANKET around her.

He LIGHTS up a cigarette, and takes a deep drag. He waits a bit.

He puts the cigarette in her mouth. She hesitates, looks up at him, then takes a deep drag.

The door opens behind them, Victor strides into the room and stops near Sasha.

                    VICTOR
          Hey. I'm deeply sorry about what
          you just had to go through, I
          really am. If you cooperate with
          me, you'll get a nice room with a
          bed. A nice roommate. And you'll
          deal with nicer customers up on the
          fourth floor. Do you want that?

No reaction.

Victor grabs her chin and puts his face right in front of hers.

                    VICTOR (CONT'D)
          Do you prefer to stay here?

She shakes her head no.

                    VICTOR (CONT'D)
          Will you cooperate with me?

She nods.

>   VICTOR (CONT'D)
>   Say it.

>   SASHA
>   (weakly)
>   I will cooperate.

>   VICTOR
>   With us.

>   SASHA
>   With you.

>   VICTOR
>   Good.

He nods to Oscar and leaves the room.

Oscar begins to unshackle her, he starts with her ankles,
which are now bleeding. Then moves up to the wrists, he is
very close to her, and there is something both threatening
and soothing about him.

He finishes to unshackle her, for a moment, it seems like he
is about to take advantage of his position, but before that
can happen, she falls into his arms.

>   OSCAR
>   Come on. You have to walk.

He helps her stand on her feet, which seems incredibly
difficult for her.

He grabs her by the shoulders and stabilizes her, she seems
to be able to stand again.

>   OSCAR (CONT'D)
>   Come.

INT. FOURTH FLOOR CORRIDOR - NIGHT

Oscar now leads Sasha, dressed in the maid outfit, back
through the upper corridor, back toward the same room.

Everything feels eerily quiet.

INT. BATHROOM - NIGHT

Blood mixes with water by Sasha's feet as she washes herself
underneath a weak, cold shower stream.

Her body is covered in bruises and scratches, but it's her psychological wounds that are clearest on her face.

Her gaze feels empty, her expression ghost-like as she seems to be coming to terms with the fact that she has lost everything.

INT. ROOM 234 - NIGHT

Sasha exits the bathroom, wearing nothing but lingerie. She walks slowly and painfully toward the queen-size bed parallel to a window.

She walks all the way to the window, and sees only a vast forest extending on the horizon, as well as her reflection. In her underwear. *Enslaved.*

Suddenly, she begins to feel an itch on her butt, reaches down and tries to look at it in the reflection, but--

KNOCK KNOCK.

The door opens, Oscar leads in a LEAN MAN in his mid-fifties, who smiles at Sasha as he walks up to her, gauges her, then begins to unbutton his white shirt. Oscar walks out.

> LEAN MAN
> You're the new one, huh? Very cute.

Sasha hides her disgust quite well. She nods.

> LEAN MAN (CONT'D)
> Well, shall we start?

Sasha begins to undress in front of him. He watches her like a predator ready for his meal.

He lays on the bed and goes on his back as he continues to watch her.

> LEAN MAN (CONT'D)
> Get on top.

She slides over him. *This is the hardest part.*

> LEAN MAN (CONT'D)
> Good girl. Now do your magic.

She takes one deep breath, then gets to work. Her face, stone-like.

He MOANS with a raspy, icky voice.

INT. ROOM 234 - MOMENTS LATER

The lean man stands by the bed, his back to her, putting his clothes back on.

She lies on the bed, curled up. *Torn between the urge to cry and the urge to jump on that man and strangle him.*

He finishes buttoning his shirt.

> LEAN MAN
> I'll see you later, honey.

He walks off.

Sasha stays in bed. Unable to move. She looks up. Suddenly she begins to fixate something: a SMOKE DETECTOR.

The door opens. Megan strides in.

> MEGAN
> Well done, honey, I hear you did
> great work. Now, you just need to
> take one little shower, okay? You
> have five minutes until the next
> one.

She walks away.

Sasha takes one more deep breath, then gets up.

INT. CORRIDOR - DAY

Now wearing her maid outfit, Sasha strolls along the corridor, in clear PAIN from her rough night, following Oscar, quiet as ever.

Sunlight shines through a distant window, indicating the night is over.

A middle-aged WOMAN walks out of a room, dressed in sweats: she clearly has nothing to do with the organization. She and Sasha exchange a brief look.

Could this woman do anything? Would she do anything?

Sasha looks back at Oscar, who drifts slightly ahead of her, and continues to follow him.

INT. BASEMENT CORRIDOR - MOMENTS LATER

The same corridor she emerged from with Megan earlier. Just
as eerie and dark as earlier. Sunlight doesn't come all the
way down there, it stops at the first floor.

Oscar leads Sasha in front of a CELL, already inhabited by
one girl we met earlier: Elena, the soothing girl who was
watching her in the changing room.

He opens the cell with a key, and invites Sasha to get in.
She does so.

INT. CELL - CONTINUOUS

There's no privacy in there. Just bars. Inside the cell, two
bunk beds, a dirty toilet, and floor that hasn't been washed
in years.

Oscar watches Sasha from the other side of the door. He takes
out a cigarette and lights it as Sasha takes in the fact that
this is now where she is going to sleep.

                    OSCAR
          You want a drag?

Sasha turns around.

                    SASHA
          Yes.

She walks over and takes a long drag.

He takes the cigarette back.

                    OSCAR
          You're going to be doing this every
          day. We pick you up in the evening,
          bring you back in the morning. You
          did good tonight.

Sasha watches him walk away.

                    ELENA
          Hi.

Sasha turns around to look at her new roommate.

                    SASHA
          Hi.

She walks to the empty bunk bed across from Elena's.

                    ELENA
          I'm Elena.

                    SASHA
          Sasha.

                    ELENA
          Nice to meet you Sasha.

Sasha doesn't respond.

                    ELENA (CONT'D)
          Today was your first night, huh?

                    SASHA
          Yes.

                    ELENA
          You want to talk?

                    SASHA
          No.

                    ELENA
          I understand. Let me know when you
          do.

Sasha closes her eyes.

Suddenly a tear rolls down her right cheek, which she tries
to hide immediately, but Elena gets up from her bed and walks
up to her.

                    ELENA (CONT'D)
          Hey, hey, it's okay. It's okay. It
          was much worse for me on my first
          night.

Elena wraps her arms around her, but Sasha pushes her away.

                    SASHA
          I am okay.

Elena doesn't try further, and goes back to her bed as Sasha
wipes away her only tear.

INT. CELL - NIGHT

Sasha and Elena both sleep in their respective beds when
FOOTSTEPS echo in the vicinity along with the clattering of
KEYS.

Sasha opens her eyes as a key enters the cell door.

Roy, one of the security guards, opens the door and lets a teenage Chinese girl, **LIN** (16), a fragile flower crushed too early by life, inside the cell.

Lin, with a broken walk, goes for the upper bunk bed above Sasha's, throwing her a sideways look.

Roy stays at the door, his eyes focused on Lin. He closes the door behind him, takes a few steps forward, then leans down over Lin, sniffing her, smelling her.

Lin shivers, petrified. She doesn't know what to do.

Elena opens her eyes and instinctively JUMPS to him, pulls him away with all her strength, causing him to knock his head against her bunk bed.

He YELLS in pain, then SLAMS his fist into her stomach. She falls back, gasping.

Lin descends from her bed and tries to stop Roy, but Roy SLAPS her and she falls down, nearly slamming her face into Sasha's bunk bed in the process.

                    OSCAR (O.S.)
          The fuck's goin' on?

Roy immediately stops and turns to Oscar, who stands on the other side of the cell.

                    ROY
          They attacked me.

                    OSCAR
          Whatcha doin' inside the cell?

                    ROY
          Defending myself.

                    OSCAR
          Get out.

Roy hesitates for a second, then leaves the cell.

Oscar remains longer, gives Elena a nod, then walks away.

Elena walks over to Lin to check on her.

                    ELENA
          You okay?

                    LIN
          Yeah. Thank you.

Elena helps Lin get up.

                    LIN (CONT'D)
          Who is this?

                    ELENA
          This is Sasha.

                    LIN
          Nice to meet you, Sasha. I am Lin,
          from China.

She waits for Sasha to respond, but she just nods and turns
away from them.

Lin looks at Elena, trying to see if she said something
wrong.

                    ELENA
          She is still shocked, I think.

Lin goes back to her bunk bed. Each of them lays quietly on
their bed, trying and failing to go back to sleep.

                    LIN
          Elena?

                    ELENA
          Yes?

                    LIN
          I thinking today: what I do if I
          not here? Do you know what you do?

                    ELENA
          I would try to be a nurse, and send
          money to my family. That was the
          plan.

                    LIN
          You still have family?

                    ELENA
          Yes, back in Colombia.

She pauses.

                    ELENA (CONT'D)
          What would you do?

                    LIN
          I want go back to school.

Both Elena and Sasha tear up, but Sasha hides it from the
other two.

                    LIN (CONT'D)
          Why you crying?

                    ELENA
          Nothing Lin. We should go back to
          sleep now.

                    LIN
          Can you sing me a song?

Elena tries to smile.

                    ELENA
          Sure. Which one?

                    LIN
          One you always sing.

Elena begins to SING a traditional Colombian lullaby in a
sweet, caring voice. Now Lin is the one tearing up, but she
soon closes her eyes.

INT. CELL - DAY

Sasha opens her eyes, one can tell it's the morning as a slit
of light shines through the cell from the top of the wall,
illuminating the room just slightly more than at night.

She turns to Elena and notices she's already awake. Elena
smiles at her.

                    ELENA
          Sleep okay?

Sasha nods.

                    ELENA (CONT'D)
          You get used to it. Sleep is best
          part of day now.

Lin moves above Sasha's bed.

                    LIN
          What you dream about?

                    ELENA
          I dream that I was flying, above
          ocean.
                    (MORE)

> ELENA (CONT'D)
> I was a small bird, and there was
> falcons following me, but then, I
> get shot by hunter, and I wake up.
> You?

> LIN
> I dream my parents still alive, and
> take me to school, but I arrive
> naked, everyone make fun of me, and
> I try to run away, but other
> students catch me and bring me back
> to school, force me to stay the
> whole day, naked.

A moment of silence.

> LIN (CONT'D)
> Sasha, you dream?

> SASHA
> No.

INT. CHANGING ROOM - DAY

A few GIRLS change into fresh maid outfits as Sasha, Lin and
Elena enter the changing room. Elena and Lin start to undress
as if it were nothing.

Elena turns to Sasha.

> ELENA
> Sasha, you need to change.

Sasha nods and begins to undress as well.

Lin grabs Sasha's dirty outfit, puts it in a large laundry
basket, and brings her a fresh one.

Sasha grabs it.

> SASHA
> You not need to do that.

> LIN
> I know.

> SASHA
> You should stay away from me.

> LIN
> Why?

Sasha just ignores her.

INT. FOURTH FLOOR CORRIDOR - MOMENTS LATER

Elena, Lin and Sasha walk together through the fourth floor, without any escort.

Sasha looks up and finally notices CAMERAS at every corner of the corridor.

Elena stops in front of 211. She takes a deep breath, then uses her key card to enter the room.

>   ELENA
>   See you.

Lin and Sasha continue quietly.

>   LIN
>   We going to be okay.

Sasha glances at her.

>   SASHA
>   Yes.

Lin stops in front of 227. Like Elena, she takes a deep breath, but it is much weaker.

>   LIN
>   See you.

Sasha nods as Lin enters her room, and she continues alone, weakly, all the way to 234, where she, also, inserts her key and enters.

INT. CELL - NIGHT

Sasha, Lin and Elena are now back on their beds, each of them staring at the ceiling.

>   LIN
>   Elena?

>   ELENA
>   Yeah?

>   LIN
>   You think we can escape?

>   ELENA
>   One day.

>   LIN
>   When?

                         ELENA
              When the right time comes.

                         SASHA
              It will never come.

     Both Elena and Lin turn to Sasha, surprised she spoke.

                         ELENA
              How do you know? You have been here
              two weeks.

                         SASHA
              I know.

     Silence.

                         ELENA
              Maybe.

                         LIN
              I don't think I can do this for
              long time.

     Another silence.

                         LIN (CONT'D)
              Sasha?

     No response.

                         LIN (CONT'D)
              Sasha?

                         SASHA
              Yes.

                         LIN
              Why you never tell us anything?

                         SASHA
              I have nothing to say.

     Lin climbs down the bed.

                         LIN
              Come on. I am sure you have things
              to tell us. How you get here?

                         SASHA
              I don't want to talk about it.

                         LIN
               It is okay. I can tell you how I
               get here. I--

Sasha grabs her throat.

                         SASHA
               I don't want to know. Go back to
               your bed, stay away from me.

She releases her. Lin, slightly shocked, goes back on the
upper bed.

                         ELENA
               She is just trying to talk, you
               know?

Footsteps. One person. Roy shows up at the door, with a
chocolate bar. All the girls fall silent and pretend to
sleep.

                         ROY
               Hey there.

He smiles, then opens the door and walks into the room.

                         ROY (CONT'D)
               Missed me?

He approaches Lin, who continues to pretend to be asleep.

                         ROY (CONT'D)
               I brought you a gift.

He waves his chocolate bar, then throws it on top of Lin. She
remains motionless.

                         ROY (CONT'D)
               It's okay. You can keep it.

He leans on her bed, next to her.

He starts running his hand along Lin's belly. Elena opens her
eyes.

                         ELENA
               Get away from her.

                         ROY
               Shut up.

Suddenly, Lin pushes away Roy's hand away, that's all she can
muster as tears start pouring out of her eyes.

                    LIN
          Go away.

                    ROY
          What does it matter to you? I can
          just be like any other client.

                    LIN
          I don't know.

                    ROY
          Come on.

He grabs her wrist, ready to attack.

Lin tries to push him away. He's too strong.

He JUMPS on top of her, one hand on her mouth.

Sasha hears from below, she tries to contain herself.

Elena gets up from her bed and starts to attack Roy, and like
last time, Roy pushes her away violently.

Lin continues to struggle with him, but he is stronger and
dominates her fully.

Lin starts to WHIMPER loudly, her mouth still gagged by Roy's
mouth.

Elena struggles to get up, then attempts to stop him one more
time, grabbing his leg and wrestling with it to pull him
away.

She gets kicked one more time as Sasha continues to struggle
internally.

Sasha suddenly gets up, SNATCHES his baton away from him, and
STRIKES him in the head with it.

He falls from the bed onto the floor. Elena gets up, and
KICKS him in the gut. He MOANS in pain.

Elena takes the baton from Sasha, and starts to STRIKE him
with it repeatedly, hysterically, losing her senses.
Suddenly, she's making all of *them* pay through him.

Oscar appears beside them, and stops Elena.

Roy lies on the floor, barely conscious, surrounded by a pool
of his own blood.

                    OSCAR
                  (to Elena)
              What did you do?

Elena stares back at Oscar, still in a trance of bloodthirsty
revenge.

INT. CONFERENCE ROOM - MOMENTS LATER

Sasha and Lin enter a wide, low-ceilinged, windowless room.

Five dozens of GIRLS, all dressed in the same maid outfit,
sit in a circle around Elena, who is GAGGED and TIED UP to a
chair in the middle of the room.

Oscar, Megan, Pete, and Roy, who is still bleeding, are also
present.

Megan pushes Sasha and Lin to sit on two empty chairs.

The room is dead quiet, aside from Elena's muffled SOBS. She
and Sasha exchange a brief look. *Sasha knows what this is.*

The door opens behind, Victor makes a dramatic appearance.

He walks quietly to the middle of the circle as all gazes
rest on him.

                    VICTOR
              Hello everyone, thanks for waking
              up and coming here for this special
              occasion.

He looks around the room to see the reactions, to take in and
savor the anxiety in the girls surrounding him.

He turns to Elena.

                    VICTOR (CONT'D)
              Elena over here, has been a very,
              very bad girl. Anybody here wanna
              take a guess why?

No one does.

                    VICTOR (CONT'D)
              Elena, here, decided that it would
              be okay to attack Roy. She stole
              his baton from behind and beat him,
              for no reason.

He pauses. Elena and Sasha exchange a look. Sasha looks ready to get up and claim responsibility for that, but Elena's look somehow stops her.

Victor strokes Elena's hair.

                    VICTOR (CONT'D)
          If it weren't for Oscar, Roy here
          would probably be dead. Dead. So,
          let me be absolutely clear: if you
          attack him, you attack all of us.

He looks around, waiting for some sort of approval.

He stares at Sasha for a brief moment.

                    VICTOR (CONT'D)
          Now, let me just illustrate what
          happens if you attack us.

And before he even finishes talking, he takes out his gun, and SMACKS it in Elena's jaw violently enough to make her drop to the ground with her chair.

Victor takes a step toward her and KICKS her in the gut. She WHIMPERS. He KICKS her in the chin.

Blood.

The girls watch in horror, frozen. Lin looks away.

Suddenly, Sasha's breathing begins to accelerate. Something inside her begins to stir.

                    VICTOR (CONT'D)
          Anyone wants to join?

Roy joins while Pete hesitates, then walks toward Elena as Victor continues to KICK her like a soccer ball.

She continues to shriek and wail and sob, it's as horrifying to hear as it is to watch. Most of the girls look away, or hide their faces and cry all they have to cry.

The only person who keeps watching is Sasha. She takes it in. If she was dead inside, this is bringing her back to life. Megan notices and watches her.

Finally, Elena goes completely quiet. Roy and Pete keep kicking her for a bit until Victor stops them.

He crouches next to her inanimate body, feels the pulse, then goes on to close her eyes.

                         VICTOR (CONT'D)
                 I'm really sorry.

He gets up, the girls look at him, numb with terror.

                         VICTOR (CONT'D)
                 I think you girls got the point.

He walks off.

Sasha turns around to look at Oscar, who watches silently.
His expression impossible to read.

Her eyes sting like she wants to cry, but her internal rage
has taken over, preventing her to do so.

Oscar grabs a pack of cigarette from his back pocket, pulls
the lighter out of it with a cig, and lights it.

Sasha stares at Oscar's cigarette with sudden realization.
She looks at the ceiling. Another SMOKE DETECTOR.

INT. BASEMENT CORRIDOR - NIGHT

Oscar escorts Sasha and Lin back to their cell.

Lin SOBS continuously as Sasha observes Oscar in silence.

They reach their door. Oscar unlocks the door, Sasha and Lin
walk into the cell.

INT. CELL - CONTINUOUS

Sasha stops, and turns back to Oscar

                         SASHA
                 Can I have cigarette?

Oscar turns to her, then through the bars, grabs Sasha by the
collar and brings her as close to him as he can, fearsome.

                         OSCAR
                 Listen to me Sasha. I am not your
                 friend. Just because I don't abuse
                 you doesn't mean I am soft, doesn't
                 mean I even like you, is that
                 clear?

Now holding her breath, she simply nods.

                         OSCAR (CONT'D)
                 Here.

He reaches down for his pocket, which she watches carefully.
He takes out his pack, takes out one with a lighter, hands
her a cig. She grabs it. He lights it.

>   OSCAR (CONT'D)
>   Enjoy.

He lets her go, and walks away.

She takes the longest possible drag, thoughtful, as Lin wipes
her tears away and looks at her.

>   LIN
>   Can I have?

Sasha turns around and hands it to Lin.

Lin looks at Sasha hesitantly as she takes her first drag.

>   LIN (CONT'D)
>   It my fault.

Sasha gives her a sympathetic look but says nothing.

>   SASHA
>   No.

Lin suddenly turns to her, stunned.

>   LIN
>   It is, she try to help me.

>   SASHA
>   It is their fault.

>   LIN
>   But maybe, if I say nothing--

>   SASHA
>   No.

>   LIN
>   You stop him. You can stop her.

>   SASHA
>   So it is my fault?

>   LIN
>   I do not say this.

Sasha gets up and faces Lin.

>   SASHA
>   What do you say?

                    LIN
          You not even care! She die, you ask
          for cigarette

                    SASHA
          Do not tell me what I care about.

                    LIN
          You don't! You lie there, say
          nothing, like we deserve this.

Sasha SLAPS Lin. It just comes out.

Lin stares at Sasha in total disbelief. All the grief and
frustration these two have just accumulated is coming out.

Lin unexpectedly PUNCHES Sasha in the face.

Sasha grabs her THROAT. The two of them SLAM against one of
the beds and start to BRAWL furiously.

The door SLAMS open. Oscar enters and separates them like
he'd separate two little puppies.

He then SHOVES Sasha against the wall. This is the most
threatening we've seen him so far.

                    OSCAR
          You fucking kidding me? You wanna
          die too?

                    LIN
          She attack me.

                    OSCAR
          Why?

                    LIN
          We fight.

Oscar looks at Lin for an instant.

Sasha looks at Oscar as he does. An idea pops in her head.

She quickly slips her hand into Oscar's pocket. Lin seems to
notice but says nothing.

She pulls out his pack of cigarettes from him.

Oscar looks back to her.

>   OSCAR
>   You two fight again like this, I
>   will have to report it, and you
>   already know what that means.

A trace of emotion in his voice that disappears as fast as it appeared.

Sasha nods, looking genuinely scared of the sheer fierceness he suddenly displays.

He lets her go, and walks out of the room.

Lin turns to Sasha.

>   LIN
>   Why you steal them?

>   SASHA
>   What?

>   LIN
>   You know what. You can just ask
>   when you want.

>   SASHA
>   Not when I want.

Lin watches her, dubious.

Sasha gets in her bed, Lin gets in hers, above her.

Sasha stares blankly above her, thoughtful.

INT. CORRIDOR - NIGHT

Sasha and Lin walk side by side. Quiet as ever.

An unusual amount of sweat seems to be decorating Sasha's forehead. Lin notices, but says nothing.

She stops in front of her room and gets into it without saying a word.

Sasha closes her eyes briefly as she keeps going and reaches her room 234.

INT. BATHROOM - NIGHT

Sasha finishes putting on her stockings, briefly looks at herself in the mirror, takes a deep breath, then grabs Oscar's cigarette PACK from her maid outfit pocket.

INT. ROOM 234 - NIGHT

Sasha strides toward the bed, quickly places the pack underneath the bed, safely. She then looks around the room.

She grabs a chair and puts it underneath the SMOKE DETECTOR.

She checks that she can reach the smoke detector when she hears FOOTSTEPS getting close.

She quickly gets off the chair, puts it back, then JUMPS on the bed as the door opens and Megan lets in Dustin, the police officer who first raped Sasha.

He smiles like the total asshole he is. Sasha's face goes livid.

> DUSTIN
> Hey there, missed me?

She gets up, her breathing accelerating in spite of herself.

A trace of excitement appears in his eyes. He takes a few steps toward her and SLAPS her face roughly.

> DUSTIN (CONT'D)
> I asked you a question.

> SASHA
> Yes.

He puts a hand on her butt, ready to slide her panties down. She stops him gently with one hand, and starts unbuttoning his shirt with the other.

He lets her do it, suddenly intrigued.

> DUSTIN
> Taught you manners here, huh?

She nods and continues to slide down his shirt, button after button.

Then, she puts her hand on his belt. He stops her.

> DUSTIN (CONT'D)
> I don't know that I'm gonna let you
> do that.

> SASHA
> Are you afraid of me?

He smiles and takes out his GLOCK 17 and his baton. He carefully puts the gun in the night stand drawer, and the baton next to it.

He walks back to her, a big smile on his face.

She continues what she started, unbuckles his belt roughly, he MOANS in excitement.

She pulls his pants down, then gets back up, his belt in hand.

He grabs her wrist, looks at the belt, and shakes his head.

She plays dumb for a moment.

                    DUSTIN
          Let go of the belt.

She drops the belt. He smiles.

                    DUSTIN (CONT'D)
          Now turn around.

She doesn't.

                    DUSTIN (CONT'D)
          I see.

He SMACKS her in the face so hard she falls to the floor.

He DIVES onto her like a predator. She ROLLS away but not fast enough.

He LIES over her back, and GRABS both her wrists with strong hands.

She STRUGGLES to BREAK FREE. He MAINTAINS a tight grip.

Her LEGS SKATE on the floor as he tries to PENETRATE her.

                    DUSTIN (CONT'D)
          Can you fucking stop moving?

She turns her head and sees the BELT lying a few inches from her.

He sees it too, grabs the belt and THROWS it away.

That's just enough time for her to SHOVE her ELBOW into his face.

He lets out a muffled SCREAM but tries to regain control over her quickly. She manages to throw him off balance.

He ROLLS to the side, she KICKS him in the balls, hard. This time he SCREAMS.

She CRAWLS over to grab the BELT.

He JUMPS on her and grabs her legs. She's about to grab the belt when he PULLS her leg farther.

She KICKS him in the face, he still holds onto it.

He keeps PULLING, her legs finally slip out.

She grabs the belt. He BITES her ankle. She SCREAMS.

He lets go and JUMPS over her.

SLASH, she WHIPS him in the face with the BELT.

BLOOD SPLATTERS over her. HE YELLS in agony.

SWOOSH. This time she WHIPS his CROTCH.

His yells grow louder.

She quickly goes behind him, WRAPS her arm around his neck, and compresses it to stop the oxygen from reaching the brain.

He tries to resist, but she stays firm. His temples compress, his face becomes whiter as the two of them SHAKE with madness as they put all their final efforts into that struggle--

Until he stops resisting and loses consciousness.

It takes a few seconds for her to realize, she then lets go of him, falls backwards and PANTS heavily.

She looks around, suddenly realizing she's not done.

She crawls to the bed and grabs the PACK of cigarettes from below it.

She takes the desk chair, puts it below the SMOKE DETECTOR, and climbs on it. She lights a cigarette and waves it below it.

Suddenly, a deafening RING buzzes through the room, and echoes from all the surrounding rooms and corridors: she's set off the alarm.

She takes a drag of her cigarette. Then jumps down and runs to the bathroom.

INT. BATHROOM - CONTINUOUS

She dives to grab her maid outfit and puts it on faster than
lightning.

INT. ROOM 234 - CONTINUOUS

As she exits the bathroom, someone KNOCKS on the door. She
looks through the peephole, and sees LIN, waiting at the
door.

>   SASHA
>   (in Russian)
>   Fuck!

She opens the door.

>   SASHA (CONT'D)
>   What?

>   LIN
>   Let me in.

>   SASHA
>   Why?

>   LIN
>   Because I know it's you. I want go
>   with you, or I tell them.

Sasha sends her a death stare, takes a deep breath, then
moves aside to let her in.

Lin walks in, Sasha locks the door after her.

Sasha grabs Lin's arm.

>   SASHA
>   You do everything I say.

That's an order. Lin nods.

>   SASHA (CONT'D)
>   We need block door. Put what you
>   can in front of it.

Lin understands, she runs to one of the night stands and
stops over Dustin's inanimate body.

>   LIN
>   Is he--?

                         SASHA
                 No. Keep going!

Lin grabs the night stand and begins to move it.

                         SASHA (CONT'D)
                 Wait.

She goes to the night stand and grabs the GLOCK 17 from the
drawer. Lin looks at it with awe, then

Meanwhile, Sasha begins to take the sheets from the bed.

Lin continues to grab stuff to put in front of the door.

Sasha begins to TIE all the sheets together

Lin runs out of things to throw in front of the door.

                         LIN
                 What else?

                         SASHA
                 Tie sheets to bed.

Lin nods and starts to do it. Dustin begins to stir. The
alarm keeps BLARING.

Indistinct VOICES begin grow in the background.

Sasha KICKS Dustin in the balls. He MOANS in pain, half
unconscious still.

She grabs the Glock 17 and SHOOTS TWICE in opposite corners
of the window.

Walks to window.

KNOCK! KNOCK! *They're here.*

Sasha HITS THE WINDOW as hard as she can with the Glock.

One, two, three. It shatters.

She pulls on the sheets. Not strong enough. She makes another
knot.

More BANGING against the door. They're trying to force it
open.

The knot's finished. Sasha puts the Glock in her pocket.

                         SASHA (CONT'D)
                 We go now.

She shoves the sheets - about 12 feet long together - down the window.

It won't get them all the way down, but they have no choice.

Sasha CLIMBS out the window quickly, holding on to the sheet, Lin does the same.

As Lin disappears, the door CRACKS open. Oscar, Pete and Roy appear, stuck behind the stuff Lin put in front of the door.

EXT. HOTEL - NIGHT

Sasha and Lin climb down the wall as fast as they can.

Yelling coming from inside.

RIP. The sheets starting to wear down.

They slip a few feet down.

>   SASHA
>   Quick.

They accelerate.

Roy appears at the window. Grabs the sheets, pulls on them, they TEAR APART.

CRASH. Sasha and Lin SMASH into the ground.

Lin WHIMPERS, holds her ankle.

Sasha grabs her by the arm, pulls her into the woods.

>   SASHA (CONT'D)
>   We need to go, now!

EXT. WOODS - NIGHT

A dense clutter of long dark tree trunks.

Half a moon shines a faint light glittering into the two girls' eyes.

Sasha and Lin RUN for their lives.

All we hear is the RUSTLING of leaves against light footsteps, repressed PANTING, and a light breeze.

Sasha runs like an athlete, while Lin falls behind, LIMPING.

                         LIN
              Sasha!

Lin looks desperate.

Yelling grows louder fifty feet behind them.

Sasha keeps going. Focused.

FLASHLIGHTS DANCE in the background, each ray more dangerous
than the other.

                         LIN (CONT'D)
              Sasha!

Sasha looks back for a second and decides to keep going. *It's
about survival now.*

Lin TRIPS over a TREE BRANCH and FALLS to the ground.

                         LIN (CONT'D)
              Help me!

                         PETE (O.S.)
              This way!

A flashlight turns to LIN and moves toward her at a fast
pace.

Sasha turns around. Watches Lin. *She needs her.*

                         LIN
              Please!

She tries to get up but realizes she is STUCK to the branch.

Sasha freezes. *Now or never.*

                         SASHA
                    (in Russian)
              Fuck me.

She RUNS to Lin.

The FLASHLIGHT gets really close.

                         PETE (O.S.)
              Over here!

Sasha REACHES Lin. The flashlight gets closer. Lin still
struggling with the branch.

Sasha gives Lin a hand and PULLS her with all her strength.

The branch TEARS off part of her outfit, but she walks FREE.

Pete arrives where they are and points a GUN at LIN, who raises her hands.

> PETE (CONT'D)
> Freeze!

Sasha comes at him from the side and SMACKS him in the head with the BRANCH Lin fell on.

He drops down, knocked out. Lin watches him horrified as Sasha grabs Lin by the arm and pulls her with her.

> SASHA
> We can't stop here. Come on.

They RUN again. Fast. Branches and leaves crack beneath them.

The YELLS in the background grow closer still.

Suddenly, Sasha and Lin STEP into a MARSH.

SPLASH. Lin FALLS face down into the water. She SCREAMS her LUNGS out.

> OSCAR (O.S.)
> Over there!

Sasha grabs Lin's arm, pulls her up.

She sees the flashlights hitting nearby trees, she looks around, and DRAGS Lin further into the marsh.

A FEW FEET BACK INTO THE WOODS

Victor, Oscar, and Roy dash through the woods, a good distance from each other so they can cover more ground,

SWEEPING their environment with FLASHLIGHTS methodically.

Victor tracks FOOTSTEPS like a hunter.

The three of them reach the marsh. Victor STOPS and so do the others.

They look at each other. Victor gives each of them two different directions to sweep, which they immediately start.

DEEPER INTO THE MARSH

Sasha and Lin HIDE, CROUCHED as deep as they can into the water, surrounded by REEDS.

Behind them, Victor's flashlight gets closer and closer.

Sasha and Lin look at each other. Sasha NODS.

They both go UNDERWATER.

Victor shows up and SWEEPS the area with his flashlight.

We can see ripples on the water where they just were as the beam of light approaches slowly.

The ripples slowly fade out, the light gets closer...

UNDERWATER

Sasha and Lin hold their breaths, trying to be as still as they can.

ABOVE WATER

The flashlight lands where the ripples were, it is now as still as everywhere else.

                    VICTOR
          Sasha, I know you're around.

A few yards away, Sasha and Lin EMERGE quietly, INHALING short, quiet breaths.

Victor HEARS something and points his light next to them.

Lin looks like she's about to scream, Sasha covers her mouth and holds her TIGHT.

Victor keeps the light there and walks toward them.

                    VICTOR (CONT'D)
          You're in big trouble, darling.

TEARS come out of Lin's eyes.

Victor takes a few STEPS closer, he's almost onto them, close enough that he'll hear any movement they make.

Sasha pulls out the GLOCK she stole earlier, and holds it close to her, ready to use it if need be.

                    OSCAR (O.S.)
          I think I got 'em.

He turns around.

                    VICTOR
          You sure?

                    OSCAR (O.S.)
          Looks like it.

                    VICTOR
          All right.

Sasha and Lin GASP for air, Sasha keeps her weapon close by,
both of them frozen both literally and figuratively.

Victor and his flashlight keep getting farther, it looks like
they're almost safe to move, but they stay absolutely still,

Terrified.

Soon they are back in total silence and darkness.

They stay put, still.

Until they hear a WEIRD NOISE clearly coming from a non-human
source.

They look at each other.

                    SASHA
          We need to go.

Lin nods energetically.

EXT. WOODS - NIGHT

Lin and Sasha now WALK through another part of the woods,
back to dry land, despite their clothes still SOAKING WET.

It's quiet, they walk side by side, no eye or physical
contact.

                    LIN
          I know this tree, we been here
          already.

                    SASHA
          Quiet.

                    LIN
          But we lost.

Sasha stops and turns to Lin.

                    SASHA
          It is dark, all trees look same.

                        LIN
            But we lost, say it! We walk for
            hours.

                        SASHA
            We are not. I know what I am doing.

She goes back to walking.

                        LIN
            You not, we die here or they going
            find us.

                        SASHA
            They do if you keep talking.

                        LIN
            Maybe they should.

Sasha stops again.

                        SASHA
            What did you say?

                        LIN
            Nothing.

                        SASHA
            You are free to go back if you
            want.

Lin's expression changes.

                        LIN
            Sorry. I not mean it.

                        SASHA
            You ready to follow me?

Lin nods.

She resumes walking. Lin hesitates, then decides to follow
her.

A LIGHT moves across the trees in the near distance.

Lin looks at Sasha.

                        LIN
            It th--

Sasha HUSHES her with her hand.

The light is gone. Sasha walks in the direction of the light. Slow at first, then she starts RUNNING.

Lin trails behind, unsure where this is leading them.

A few dozen yards later, Sasha stops and turns to Lin.

> SASHA
> See. I know where we going.

She points at the direction they first saw the lights.

Lin approaches Sasha and sees the TREELINE stop in the direction she's pointing.

> SASHA (CONT'D)
> Come.

EXT. COUNTY ROAD - NIGHT

A local county road consisting of two narrow lanes, separates the woods at that specific point.

It's the kind of road in which you might see one car every hour if you're lucky.

Sasha and Lin emerge from the woods on the East side and walk along the road.

Lin walks practically on the actual road, looking in both directions, she raises her arm, hoping to hitchhike.

Sasha RUNS to her, GRABS her hand, and DRAGS her back into the woods.

> SASHA
> Do not do this. What if they on
> same road?

> LIN
> Why we find road if we not use it?

> SASHA
> Just follow me.

Sasha leads her to walk along the road, but from within the woods.

They go back to their mutual silence.

EXT. COUNTY ROAD - NIGHT

Sasha and Lin walk the way we left them. It's still pitch
black.

They reach a HIKING TRAIL that starts from the road. A 90's
COROLLA is parked by the trail. Empty.

Sasha stops Lin. She listens carefully, making sure they're
alone.

> SASHA
> Stay here.

She approaches the car slowly: no one is in it. She tries to
open each door. They're all locked.

She motions to Lin to come quietly. Lin obeys.

Sasha takes her gun out and HITS the CORNER of the driver's
WINDOW.

TWO SHARP HITS, the window SHATTERS into hundreds of small
pieces, Sasha takes a step back to let them fall.

> LIN
> What you doing?

> SASHA
> Surviving.

She PULLS the driver's side LOCK.

Lin watches Sasha with a mixture of awe and terror.

Sasha hands her the gun. Lin holds it like she'd hold a
spider.

> LIN
> What I do with it?

Sasha PULLS the safety and makes Lin aim to the trees. She
puts Lin's finger on the trigger.

> SASHA
> If you see one of them, you shoot.
> Otherwise, just point somewhere
> else.

Lin nods, clearly terrified at the thought of shooting.

Sasha OPENS the trunk and looks at a TOOLBOX, sitting in a corner, next to CAMPING SUPPLIES.

I/E. COROLLA - NIGHT

Sasha SHUTS the door with a SCREWDRIVER in one hand.

She INSERTS the screwdriver into the ignition, and WIGGLES it for a few seconds.

Lin watches dubiously from outside as Sasha struggles to get it in fully.

> LIN
> How you know steal car?

> SASHA
> I am not nice person.

A NOISE coming from the trees STARTLES Lin and she instantly SHOOTS at the trees.

The BANG seems to ECHO five times before it dies out.

Sasha gives Lin a cold stare.

> SASHA (CONT'D)
> When do I say, shoot trees?

> LIN
> I sorry, I--

> SASHA
> We need to get out of here now, get in!

Sasha continues to WIGGLE the screwdriver, with renewed intensity, it doesn't do anything.

> SASHA (CONT'D)
> Come on, stupid car.

Another noise comes from the woods, but this time, TWO CAMPERS emerge from them.

They stop when they see Lin and Sasha in their car.

Lin instantly raises the gun at them. They raise their hands.

Time seems to freeze as the four of them stare at each other, unclear what to do, fearing each other.

Finally, Sasha makes the engine ROAR and, again, it seems to echo for miles around, the campers keep staring.

Lin keeps pointing the gun, trembling.

Sasha gets in drive mode, and slowly DRIVES away, eyes still glued to the campers.

INT. COROLLA (MOVING) - MOMENTS LATER

Sasha stares blankly into the dark void ahead.

Lin looks around, hopelessly trying to understand it.

The eerie sound of wind pouring inside the car forces them to yell.

> LIN
> Where are we?

> SASHA
> I not sure yet.

> LIN
> Where we going?

> SASHA
> I don't know!

> LIN
> But-- we stay together, yes?

> SASHA
> For now.

Lin does her best to ignore that threat and opens the glove compartment, as if expecting to find something new there.

She also scratches her butt intensely.

> LIN
> I am hungry.

Sasha doesn't respond.

> LIN (CONT'D)
> And thirsty. And I need to pee.

> SASHA
> Why you not pee in forest?

> LIN
> I do not think about it.

                    SASHA
          I need get us far from here.

                    LIN
          I cannot hold for long.

Sasha sighs.

                    SASHA
          I do not know if you notice, Lin,
          but we have bigger problems right
          now.

Lin sighs too. She thinks.

Sasha looks into her rearview mirror.

                    SASHA (CONT'D)
               (in Russian)
          Shit.

                    LIN
          What is it?

She looks behind and sees a COP CAR driving right behind
them.

                    LIN (CONT'D)
          You think, for us?

                    SASHA
          I don't know.

                    LIN
          What should we do?

                    SASHA
          I don't know, all right? Just let
          me think.

                    LIN
          I know we should not steal car.

                    SASHA
          Oh really, and what was your great
          plan?

                    LIN
          I do not know, not that.

                    SASHA
          Yes, well at least I trying
          something here.

>   LIN
>   Great, now we go to jail.

>   SASHA
>   We are not going to jail!

>   LIN
>   Yes we do! They deport us.

>   SASHA
>   No they do not.

>   LIN
>   They do.

>   SASHA
>   Shut up!

>   LIN
>   You shut up!

>   SASHA
>   I should leave you there!

>   LIN
>   I should stay there!

At that moment, the cop car's LEDs start FLASHING.

Lin and Sasha become dead silent and watch.

Sasha slows down to pull over, when the cop car ACCELERATES and PASSES them on their left.

Sasha and Lin look at each other and SIGH in relief.

Sasha glances at Lin, who says nothing.

Her entire body is shaking though. *She's still a child.*

>   SASHA
>   I am hungry too.

Lin glances back at Sasha, still shaking.

The two of them exchange a look, then smile. *They're safe for now.*

A moment of silence. It's hard to do small talk when you're running for your life, but silence is heavy.

Lin turns on the RADIO. A country song starts to play. Not Lin's cup of tea. She tunes in to other frequencies, skips over classical music, and settles for a Latino song.

Sasha plays with the radio and brings the classical back.

The two of them play with the radio a couple times, then start to chuckle.

EXT. LUKOIL - NIGHT

A very wide gas station with green patches surrounding it.

An ATTENDANT fills up the tank for the only car around.

Sasha PULLS UP on the opposite side of the road.

INT. COROLLA - NIGHT

Sasha turns off her headlights but keeps the engine on. She opens the GLOVE COMPARTMENT and pulls out a couple twenties.

                    SASHA
          I stay here, hurry up.

Lin grabs the cash and opens the door.

EXT. LUKOIL - NIGHT

Lin CROSSES the street, heads toward the station's STORE.

INT. STORE - NIGHT

Lin enters, her outfit still wet, dirty, ripped, her arms covered in SCRATCHES.

The CASHIER (24), total nerd, only person in the store, looks at her, puzzled.

                    LIN
          Where is bathroom?

The cashier points to the sign, still trying to figure out what the hell just walked in.

INT. COROLLA - NIGHT

Sasha looks around. It's completely dead. She lets her head lean against the head rest, and adjusts the central mirror.

She looks at the store through the window, then looks at the lever.

She looks around, then puts the lever in drive. She looks out the window one more time.

OUT THE WINDOW

A WHITE HONDA ACCORD pulls up into the gas station.

INT. STORE BATHROOM - NIGHT

Lin uses tap water to try and CLEAN her arms and face.

She looks into the mirror, and notices her eyes are BLOODSHOT.

INT. COROLLA - NIGHT

OUT THE WINDOW

The Accord's window goes down and reveals OSCAR in the driver's seat.

The attendant goes to talk to him.

INSIDE

Sasha's LIPS tremble. She puts her hand on the selection LEVER and goes to Neutral.

INT. STORE - NIGHT

Lin walks through the AISLE, deciding what to pick. She hesitates between a CHOCOLATE BAR and a pack of CANDIES.

INT. COROLLA - NIGHT

OUT THE WINDOW

Oscar gets out of the car as the attendant pulls the PUMP.

Roy and Pete join him and they walk toward the store. No sign of Victor.

INSIDE

Sasha goes into drive.

INT. STORE - NIGHT

Lin puts a small pile of ITEMS on the REGISTER.

The cashier looks at her and slowly starts to SCAN them.

EXT. LUKOIL - NIGHT

Oscar and the others approach the store.

They slow down as they can now see Lin through the window.

Roy and Pete walk ahead of Oscar and unholster their GUNS.

THROUGH THE WINDOW

Lin grabs her PLASTIC BAG and turns to exit. She FREEZES when she sees the three men facing her.

OUTSIDE

The three men also stop.

They look at each other. Roy and Pete slowly raise their GUNS to her.

Suddenly, the sound of a ROARING ENGINE comes from the side.

Oscar turns to look at where it comes from.

BOOM!

The Corolla SLAMS into Roy and Pete and comes to a halt.

They FLY in the air and ROLL on the ground, knocked out.

Sasha points her GLOCK at Oscar through the window. She does her best to prevent her arm from shaking.

Oscar holds his gun to the side.

> SASHA
> Drop it.

Oscar doesn't budge.

> OSCAR
> You're not gonna shoot me.

BANG! Sasha SHOOTS just a little bit off Oscar's right.

> SASHA
> Are you sure?

> OSCAR
> Sasha, if you come back now, you
> might stay alive.

                          SASHA
               Drop it or I not miss this time.

Oscar sighs. He drops his gun slowly.

                          OSCAR
               Where are you going to go? The cops
               are with us.

                          SASHA
               Lin?
                    (to Oscar)
               Drop your car keys and wallet.

Lin comes out. He drops his car keys.

                          SASHA (CONT'D)
                    (to Lin)
               Get keys, wallet and guns.

Lin quickly grabs them.

                          SASHA (CONT'D)
               Now lie on floor, face down.

Oscar doesn't move.

                          SASHA (CONT'D)
               You hear what I say? Lie. Down.

Oscar looks at her defiantly, but does it anyway.

Sasha turns off the engine, gets out of the car, leans next
to Oscar, and KNOCKS him out with the back of her Glock.

                          SASHA (CONT'D)
               Let's go.

INT. ACCORD (MOVING) - MOMENTS LATER

Lin looks at Sasha, trying to gauge how mad she is.

                          LIN
               Thank you.

Sasha doesn't respond. Lin opens the chocolate bar and hands
Sasha a piece of chocolate. She drinks a long gulp of water.

                          LIN (CONT'D)
               But how they know we were there?

Sasha looks at her.

                        SASHA
          I don't know.

   Lin grabs another piece of chocolate.

                        LIN
          Sasha?

                        SASHA
          Yes?

                        LIN
          Can I ask you question?

                        SASHA
          Yes.

                        LIN
          You say you not good person before.

   She hesitates.

                        LIN (CONT'D)
          Why?

   Sasha hesitates too.

                        SASHA
          I do bad things back home.

                        LIN
          Like what?

                        SASHA
          You not want to know.

                        LIN
          I do.

                        SASHA
          I tell you later.

   Lin takes another piece of chocolate.

   They revert back to silence. Lin ITCHES her butt in a frantic
   way.

                        LIN
          My butt hurt.

   Sasha looks at her and suddenly notices SWEAT dripping on
   Lin's forehead.

   She BRAKES violently.

The car comes to a stop. Sasha turns to Lin.

> SASHA
> Show me.

> LIN
> What?

> SASHA
> Your ass, show me.

Lin looks at her, bewildered, she slides her outfit up to show her butt, where she appears to have a bruise around a small SCAR.

Sasha lifts her outfit up as well and shows Lin her butt.

> SASHA (CONT'D)
> Do I have scar there?

Lin sees a SCAR that looks very similar to hers.

> LIN
> I think.

They look at each other, suddenly understanding.

EXT. COUNTY ROAD - MOMENTS LATER

Sasha BREAKS her right side view MIRROR with the back of her gun. The mirror SHATTERS into small pieces.

She grabs the biggest one and opens the back door.

> SASHA
> Come here.

Lin gets out of the car. Sasha hands her the piece of glass.

> SASHA (CONT'D)
> You need cut around my scar with
> this.

The horror on Lin's face makes everything else so far look like a smile.

> LIN
> No.

> SASHA
> I need you to do it. Please.

                    LIN
          But--

                    SASHA
          No buts, do you want to survive?

                    LIN
          Yes but you can do it on me!

                    SASHA
          What if nothing is there? I don't
          want infect you for no reason, you
          have to do it on me first, to make
          sure.

Lin freezes.

                    SASHA (CONT'D)
          Now Lin!

                    LIN
          Okay.

Sasha bends over to support herself on the backseat, and
pulls up her outfit.

Lin leans over, and tries to INSERT the piece of glass into
Sasha's skin, right next to the scar.

The glass CUTS through. BLOOD comes out and DRIPS along
Sasha's butt.

Lin WHIMPERS at the sight of the blood.

                    LIN (CONT'D)
          I cannot do this.

                    SASHA
          Yes you can, you done hard part,
          now keep cutting.

Multiple TEARS come out of Lin's eyes. She SLOWLY CUTS around
Sasha's SCAR. BLOOD all over her fingers. Sasha GULPS
multiple times, but holds the screams.

                    SASHA (CONT'D)
          Now look for small piece of metal.

                    LIN
          Inside?

She looks like she's about to faint.

                         SASHA
                  Yes, inside.

Lin whimpers, and inserts a TREMBLING hand inside the fresh
wound. Sasha CRIES in pain. Lin finally FINDS something and
pulls out a small METALLIC CHIP: *a tracking device.*

Lin holds it in her hand, frozen, horrified.

Sasha hoists herself up and turns around. She grabs the
tracking device and throws it away.

                         SASHA (CONT'D)
                  Your turn.

                         LIN
            Now?

                         SASHA
            Now.

Lin takes a deep breath, hands the piece of glass to Sasha,
courageously turns around, and bares her butt.

                         SASHA (CONT'D)
                  I start now, okay?

Lin nods quickly, already holding her breath, closing her
eyes.

                         SASHA (CONT'D)
                  Talk to me.

Sasha gently inserts the piece of glass in Lin's butt. Blood
begins to flow down.

                         LIN
                  What you want to talk?

Sasha continues to cut. Lin holds her screams.

                         SASHA
            Anything.

                         LIN
            You have pet?

                         SASHA
            I had cat. Begemot.

She cuts some more. This time, Lin CRIES a little.

                         LIN
                  I always want cat.

                         SASHA
                    I miss him.

She puts her finger inside, looking for the tracking device.

                         LIN
                    What happen to him?

Sasha takes out the tracking device.

                         SASHA
                    Here you go.

She shows Lin the tracking device.

Lin finally breathes. Sasha RIPS off part of her outfit to
wrap around Lin's wound.

                         LIN
                    Thank you.

                         SASHA
                    Come on. We need to go.

                         LIN
                    Where we going?

                         SASHA
                    I don't know.

INT. ACCORD (MOVING) - NIGHT

Sasha turns the engine back on, and floors the gas.

Lin presses on her wound and moans softly.

                         SASHA
                    You were brave back there.

                         LIN
                    Thank you.

                         SASHA
                    Lin?

                         LIN
                    Yes?

                         SASHA
                    I sorry I yelled at you.

Lin smiles.

                         LIN
                    I sorry too.

Sasha puts her hand on Lin's for a few seconds. She looks at
the time: it reads 5:26 AM.

                         SASHA
                    Everyone asleep.

Lin looks at Sasha quizzically.

                         LIN
                    Do you have family?

                         SASHA
                    Yes.

                         LIN
                    You have brother or sister?

                         SASHA
                    Sister.

                         LIN
                    You miss her?

                         SASHA
                    I do.

Silence.

A tear escapes Lin's eye.

                         LIN
                    I have no family.

Sasha tries to keep it together. Now she really feels sorry
for her. She puts her hand on Lin's.

                         SASHA
                    Now you have me.

The two of them swallow that for a moment.

                         SASHA (CONT'D)
                    How much in wallet?

Lin checks the wallet they stole from Oscar. She pulls out a
few bills and counts them.

                         LIN
                    Two hundred, forty three dollars.

                    SASHA
         That is enough for now.

EXT. BELLEVILLE MOTOR LODGE - DAWN

The Accord pulls up into the parking lot.

INT. ACCORD - CONTINUOUS

Lin looks at Sasha anxiously.

                    LIN
         You no think they find us here?

                    SASHA
         We don't have tracking now.

Lin still looks worried.

Sasha opens the door.

                    SASHA (CONT'D)
         Come on.

INT. BELLEVILLE MOTOR LODGE - DAWN

Sasha and Lin stride in. They're a sight to behold. Dry blood
along their legs. Torn, light clothes. Dirt all over. With
only a plastic bag in their hands.

A half-asleep RECEPTIONIST appraises them from head to tow.

                    RECEPTIONIST
         What do you want?

                    SASHA
         One room. Two bed.

                    RECEPTIONIST
         You can pay?

Sasha pulls the wallet stolen from Oscar.

                    SASHA
         How much?

                    RECEPTIONIST
         Forty-five bucks for the night. You
         pay up-front.

Sasha puts sixty bucks on the counter.

                         SASHA
                 So you no ask questions.

The receptionist counts the money and makes a face.

                      SASHA (CONT'D)
                 Do you have clean clothes?

                      RECEPTIONIST
                 This is a motel, not Goodwill.

Sasha adds another twenty.

                         SASHA
                 Please?

                      RECEPTIONIST
                 You hear what I say, lady?

Sasha puts one more twenty.

                         SASHA
                 This all we have.

He looks at the extra cash. Looks at poor Lin who's never
seemed so desperate. Sighs.

                      RECEPTIONIST
                 We might've some old shit lying
                 around. I'll check it out and bring
                 it to ya.

He grabs a key off the wall and puts it on the counter.

                   RECEPTIONIST (CONT'D)
                 Room Twenty-four.

                         SASHA
                 Thank you.

She grabs the key and walks off. Lin follows behind.

INT. ROOM 24 - MOMENTS LATER

Sasha and Lin walk into the room, close the door behind them.
The room looks oddly similar to the rooms from the other
hotel.

Lin freezes.

Sasha looks at her and gets it.

> SASHA
> It's okay Lin. We free.

She puts her arm around her, and gently pushes her forward.

> SASHA (CONT'D)
> Here, you get some rest.

Lin nods, moves forward, then stops.

> LIN
> I want wash first.

Sasha smiles.

> SASHA
> Good idea.

She puts their plastic bag carefully on one of the beds. Then guides Lin to the bathroom, and turns the tap on.

> SASHA (CONT'D)
> Enjoy.

> LIN
> Can you stay with me?

> SASHA
> I will be right here.

> LIN
> Okay.

Sasha nods gets out of the bathroom.

She slowly goes to one of the beds and crashes on top of it. Her eyes close.

INT. ROOM 24 - MOMENTS LATER

KNOCK. KNOCK.

Sasha's eyes open. Her body flies up.

She looks around. Nothing.

KNOCK. KNOCK.

Sasha grabs her gun and walks carefully toward the door, one quiet step at a time.

KNOCK. KNOCK. KNOCK.

She leans in to look through the peephole.

Suddenly, the bathroom door OPENS and STARTLES Sasha, who
JUMPS and points her gun at...

Lin, in a bathrobe. Lin SCREAMS. Sasha DROPS the gun and
CATCHES it right before it hits the floor.

>   LIN
>   Sorry, I not--

>   SASHA
>   All good.

KNOCK. KNOCK.

>   RECEPTIONIST (O.S.)
>   Hello? Anyone here?

Sasha turns around and opens the door.

>   RECEPTIONIST (CONT'D)
>   Here.

The receptionist hands her two folded outfits.

Sasha inspects them, it's basically a white shirt, a skirt, a
sweater and tights.

The receptionist motions to leave.

>   SASHA
>   No shoes?

>   RECEPTIONIST
>   There's slippers in the bathroom.

He walks away. She closes the door.

INT. ROOM 24 - MOMENTS LATER

Sasha and Lin both lie inside their beds, comfortably tucked
in. *This is the first time they get to sleep in a real bed.*

They're both more than ready to sleep, but somehow, they're
terrified of it.

>   LIN
>   What we do now?

                    SASHA
          I call consulate for you. We have
          appointment tomorrow. Maybe they
          help you.

                    LIN
          And you?

                    SASHA
          I have business in Ukraine.

                    LIN
          You leave me alone?

                    SASHA
          Not alone.

                    LIN
          But you leave me.

                    SASHA
          With better people.

                    LIN
          I don't want to be with other
          people.

                    SASHA
          It is not your decision.

Lin thinks for a moment.

                    LIN
          Sasha?

                    SASHA
          Yes?

                    LIN
          What happen to your sister?

Sasha looks at her and hesitates for a moment.

                    SASHA
          She is dead.

                    LIN
          Sorry, I--.

                    SASHA
          It is because of me.

Lin turns to her, unsure what to say.

                    SASHA (CONT'D)
          She is dead because of me.

                    LIN
          I not believe that.

                    SASHA
          I do bad things in Ukraine-- for
          money. I want--

                    LIN
          What bad things?

                    SASHA
          I-- move drug money through Russian
          border.

She hesitates.

                    SASHA (CONT'D)
          I do it for her. Save money to move
          to America. She decide to learn
          with me. I say no. She insist. I
          let her do it. But she is too young
          to do this. One day, she makes big
          mistake, and they kill her.

The realization is strangely chilling to her.

She turns around to look at Lin's reaction: she's sleeping.

Sasha goes back. A tear escapes her, and she closes her eyes.

INT. ROOM 24 - DUSK

Rays of golden sunlight penetrate the room and hit Sasha's face as she opens her eyes groggily.

She hasn't slept so well in a long time.

She looks to her left: Lin's still fast asleep, curled up on her side, clutching her pillow. Sasha smiles.

She gets up, grabs the remaining pile of clothes left (she was sleeping in her shirt).

Also grabs the plastic bag with the handguns in it, and walks to the bathroom.

INT. BATHROOM - NIGHT

A weak stream of hot water hits Sasha's face. Pure heaven.

She slowly and carefully massages herself and does her best to clean the many SCRATCHES that are all over her.

MOMENTS LATER

Sasha finishes buttoning her shirt.

BAM!

Somebody just kicked open the room's main door.

Sasha trembles.

Confused muffled noises.

Footsteps.

Flashback images of her previous kidnapping.

Now Lin screaming in the room. *They found us.*

Fear and rage of her face. She looks down.

Someone wiggling the bathroom doorknob.

She looks around:

A window.

The doorknob wiggling intensely.

Sasha opens the window, it's tight. She carefully hops over it.

The door BANGS open.

Sasha's gone.

EXT. BELLEVILLE MOTOR LODGE - NIGHT

Sasha RUNS along the side of the motel toward a small patch of trees.

Only a few meters, she goes and hides behind a tree.

Roy comes out her room's window and jumps down. He looks to both sides, decides the trees are a stronger bet.

He walks over as she hides behind a large trunk.

Roy stops right behind that same trunk. Looking around. Moving his flashlight across the trees, it feels like deja-vu.

                    ROY
                (into walkie)
        I lost Sasha, I'm following a lead
        now. She can't go far.

He holsters his walkie. Then takes a few steps forward.

                    ROY (CONT'D)
        Sasha? I know you're here.
        Someone's been a bad, bad girl.

CRUNCH. Sasha SLAMS her foot into his KNEE. He YELLS and
PUNCHES her back in the face.

She STUMBLES and FALLS.

He DIVES onto her, but she KICKS him in the head as he does,
and he FALLS to the side, unconscious.

She checks him, then looks up:

Oscar and Pete lead a semi-conscious Lin into a car.

Sasha's breathing accelerates. She remains hidden.

Roy's walkie starts to produce static.

                    OSCAR (V.O.)
                (from walkie)
        Roy, you copy?

Static stops.

                    OSCAR (V.O.)
        Roy, do you copy?

Sasha looks between Roy and the car Oscar's in. *She can't
stay where she is.*

She takes the walkie, Roy's holster and gun, and runs off.

EXT. BACKYARDS - NIGHT

Sasha runs for her life from one private wooden area to
another.

She stops to catch her breath. Then thinks.

She can hear police sirens in the background. She looks
around:

Everything else is quiet.

They could come at her at any point.

She continues to catch her breath. *She needs to lay low for a while.*

She looks around one more time: a BOAT lying in the adjacent backyard. *It's her chance.*

She runs to the boat: it's covered. She unties the cover on the side, begins to climb.

CREAK, the boat moves slightly. She stops.

Total silence.

She resumes climbing, and ends up inside the boat, which she tightens from the inside.

INT. BOAT - NIGHT

Sasha continues to breathe fast. *She's now completely alone.*

> SASHA
> (in Russian, whispering to
>   herself)
> Come on Sasha, Get. Your. Shit.
> Together.

Her breathing slows down as she talks.

Until it becomes normal again.

She notices her hand still clutching the gun she stole from Dustin apparently for the first time.

> SASHA (CONT'D)
> (same)
> Daria. I'm so sorry. I know. Lin.

She begins to cry. She looks slightly insane in that moment.

> SASHA (CONT'D)
> (same)
> Yes. You can do this. You can do
> this. You can do this. Just wait.

She takes a deep breath.

> SASHA (CONT'D)
> (her lips move but
>   practically no sound
>   comes out)
> (MORE)

>   SASHA (CONT'D)
>   Three Thousand Six Hundred, Three
>   Thousand Five Hundred and Ninety
>   Nine, Three Thousand Five Hundred
>   and Ninety Eight...

INT. BOAT - MOMENTS LATER

Sasha, in the same position, looking more determined than
ever.

>   SASHA
>   (same)
>   ...Eight, Seven, Six, Five, Four,
>   Three, Two, One.

She stops.

She sits up, and carefully lifts the cover just enough to
make a slit she can see through.

Still nothing. Exactly as she left it.

No more police sirens though.

They gave up, for now.

She lifts it up more, grabs her piece, then climbs out of it.

EXT. STREET - NIGHT

A neighboring street. Suburban dead.

Sasha sticks out like a sore thumb, walking around there.

No cars so far. She keeps walking.

An old E-Class finally drives by. Sasha casually walks in
front of it and lifts her gun-free hand.

The car stops. She walks to the driver's window.

The DRIVER (25), visibly drunk, not insensitive to her
physical appearance, rolls it down.

>   DRIVER
>   Anything I can help you with Miss?

>   SASHA
>   You can drive me somewhere?

>   DRIVER
>   Hop in.

INT. E-CLASS - NIGHT

Sasha closes the door. The driver looks at her a little too happily.

> DRIVER
> Where to, sweetheart?

> SASHA
> You from here?

He smiles, looks a little taken aback, and hands it to her. He finally notices that Sasha is armed, and STARTS a bit.

> DRIVER
> You some kind of cop?

> SASHA
> No.

> DRIVER
> Oh shit, you gonna kill me?

She COCKS the gun.

> SASHA
> You from here?

> DRIVER
> Ye- Yeah, born and raised.

> SASHA
> Know the area?

> DRIVER
> Yeah, there ain't that much--

> SASHA
> You know hotel next to forest?

> DRIVER
> I'm not entirely--

> SASHA
> It is also brothel.

He looks sideways at her.

> DRIVER
> Ah, so you *are* a cop.

Sasha pushes the barrel against his neck.

                              DRIVER (CONT'D)
                    Okay, okay, there's only one
                    brothel around here, and it is next
                    to a forest: the Fair Field.

                              SASHA
                    Take me there.

EXT. INTERSTATE 80 - NIGHT

The E-Class drives along and almost empty road.

INT. E-CLASS - NIGHT

The driver and Sasha sit next to each other quietly.

                              SASHA
                    How far are we?

                              DRIVER
                    I'd say about half a mile.

                              SASHA
                    Leave me here.

                              DRIVER
                    What, in the middle of the--

                              SASHA
                    Yes.

                              DRIVER
                    Okay.

He pulls over, she exits.

EXT. FOREST - NIGHT

We're back in the forest, the same one she was running
through with Lin a day before.

Now she's walking by herself, with nothing but a gun in her
hand and a the face of ultimate determination.

She moves through the uneven ground, leaves and branches on
the ground like a terminator. *Nothing's gonna stop her now.*

As we get closer to her though, we can see her breathing
accelerating.

If we looked even closer, we'd see her pulse beating through her temple. Matching the rhythm of her footsteps.

EXT. THE FAIR FIELD - NIGHT

Sasha approaches the edge of the forest.

She gets a glimpse of the hotel for the first time: Four stories of concrete, a few lit windows like eyes in the dark, observing her.

She stops at the edge and looks around. No sign of activity outside. She notices a few cameras lining up the walls around the first floor.

She takes a few steps back, then walks along the treeline to go along the cameras' dead angle.

She then runs toward the closest wall, and leans against it.

She slides against the wall until she lands right next to a LIT WINDOW. She takes a very quick and very discreet peak inside:

THROUGH THE WINDOW

Roy and Pete sit behind monitors, stuffing their faces with Fast Food.

OUTSIDE

She takes a deep breath, then HITS the window with the back of her gun.

She stands against the wall right next to it. Waiting.

CLICK. Window gets unlocked, and raised.

Roy's face comes out the window. He looks to his right.

SMACK. The back of her gun against his skull. Knocked out instantly.

He goes LIMP.

                    PETE (O.S.)
          Shit. Roy, what's going on man?

Footsteps. Roy's body gets dragged inside the room.

Sasha takes another deep breath, then FLIPS to face the window.

THROUGH THE WINDOW

Pete HOLDS Roy in his arms, trying to feel a pulse.

He looks up and sees...

OUTSIDE

Sasha, pointing her gun at him. SHAKING. Hushing him with her other hand.

THROUGH THE WINDOW

He raises his arms and lets Roy slide down.

She motions for him to get closer. He obeys.

                    SASHA
          Turn around.

His back to her. So tall he's still threatening.

She does to him what she did to Roy. He falls down.

She CLIMBS over the window.

INT. SECURITY ROOM - NIGHT

Sasha stands above Roy and Pete's bodies.

She now has access to the monitors they were watching. A few dozen screens.

ON SCREEN

All the corridors of the hotel are covered. Also the basement, and all the rooms the girls are staying in. Finally, she can see Lin SHACKLED in the black room, sleeping.

ON SASHA

Her jaw and temple tense up when she sees Lin.

She looks around. On the table is a series of floor plans of the hotel, level by level.

She grabs all of them and scans them with her eyes.

She looks back at the guards, who begin to STIR. She KICKS both of them in the head.

She crouches next to them, grabs their handcuffs, and handcuffs both of them.

She then takes their shirts off and GAGS them with them.

She grabs one of the guards' WALKIES, KEYCARDS, BELTS (which includes baton, gun, flashlight, etc.), SHOES, puts the surveillance on, and exits the room.

INT. CORRIDOR - NIGHT

Sasha walks through the ground floor corridors. She makes a right turn. Another right.

Anyone can walk in on her and all will be over.

She moves quickly.

A few more steps. Then, the door she was looking for.

A key SWIPE. BEEP. She's in. She closes her eyes in relief.

INT. BREAKER BOX ROOM - NIGHT

A low, eerie hum fills the otherwise barren room.

A TOOLBOX lies on the floor.

On the wall, an abnormally large BREAKER BOX connected to WIRES that go up the wall.

Sasha opens the breaker box. Labels next to each FUSE read - *General 1st Floor, Dining Room, Reception, etc.*

Each Floor has its general switch, and then sub-switches.

She takes a deep breath, then turns off each general switches, starting from the fourth floor all the way down to the basement.

A HUM every time she turns a switch off.

Then total darkness.

Static on the radio.

> OSCAR (V.O.)
> (from walkie)
> What the fuck's going on down here?

No response. Sasha turns on a flashlight, opens the toolbox, and grabs a HAMMER.

                              OSCAR (V.O.)
                    Guys, do you copy?

She begins to HAMMER the box, specifically around the First
Floor and Basement General Fuses.

                              MEGAN (V.O.)
                    I copy.

                              PORTER (V.O.)
                    I copy.

SPARKLES fly in. She HAMMERS with FURY, enough to wake people
around her.

                              OSCAR (V.O.)
                    What the fuck is that ruckus?
                    Anybody has eyes on Roy and Porter?

                              MEGAN (V.O.)
                    Nope. Want us to go up there? I'm
                    on duty.

                              PORTER (V.O.)
                    I can go.

                              OSCAR (V.O.)
                    Thanks Porter. Keep us posted.

Sasha smiles. *She can take them.*

She grabs the first floor's floor plan, shines the flashlight
on it, then folds it and pockets it.

She holsters her Flashlight and opens the door.

INT. CORRIDOR - NIGHT

The corridors are all dark now, aside from the dim
illumination coming from a few exit signs here and there.

Enough to give Sasha her bearings. She walks to the left, and
goes back toward where she came from: the security room.

Ahead of her, she can hear quick FOOTSTEPS coming from a
perpendicular corridor. She accelerates, then stops at the
corner.

FOOTSTEPS growing louder, a flashlight hits the door and
intensifies. Her breathing growing faster.

She stands, frozen, and takes out her baton slowly. SWEAT
drips down her forehead.

PORTER (39) the hotel receptionist, walks straight to the security door, he doesn't see her. He KNOCKS.

> PORTER
> Anybody there?

Sasha takes several quiet steps toward him, clutching her baton harder than ever.

He opens the door, sees the two BODIES on the floor.

She JUMPS on him, he suddenly hears her, turns around, and BLOCKS her baton in midair.

She SLAMS her body against him and PUSHES him against the door.

He tries to take the baton away from her, she maintains her grip, the two wrestle quietly in the dark.

He HEADBUTTS her nose, she staggers backwards and DROPS the baton.

As he takes his gun out, she TACKLES him one more time. He falls and drops the gun.

They land next to the baton, his face at the threshold.

He tries to reach for the baton. She SLAMS her knee into his balls to stop him, then hoists herself up, grabs the edge of the door, and SLAMS it against his HEAD.

BAM. BAM. BAM. BAM.

She stops and sees a stream of blood escape from his temple. He's knocked out all right.

She steps off him and goes against the wall for a moment, trying to catch her breath.

> OSCAR (V.O.)
> Porter, what's your update?

This takes her out of her reverie.

> OSCAR (V.O.)
> Porter, do you copy?

She quickly gets up, grabs Porter and pulls him inside.

INT. SECURITY ROOM - CONTINUOUS

She handcuffs Porter and gags him the same way as the other two.

As soon as she stops, everything's become very quiet. *Too quiet.*

She hesitates - *leaving now might mean exposing herself.*

She decides to hide underneath the DESK. Cocks her gun.

She waits there, clutching her gun. Eyes closed to stay calm.

                    SASHA
               (to herself)
        Come on. Come. Come.

Finally, the door SLAMS open.

She opens her eyes.

A few footsteps. Feet appear in Sasha's view.

A flashlight's halo moves around the room, and comes dangerously close to her. She raises the gun.

Suddenly, someone crouches down, Megan's face appears right in front of her.

BAAANG.

BLOOD explodes out of Megan's face. She falls down immediately.

Sasha CRAWLS out from the desk, gets up and...

BANG, another shot, on her this time. In her THIGH.

She drops her gun and drops down as blood begins to pour out her bullet wound. She tries to scream but no sound comes out.

In front of her stand OSCAR and VICTOR.

She tries to get up, but falls again as Oscar takes a few steps toward her, pulls her gun away, then hoists her up onto his shoulder.

                    VICTOR
        Told ya.

He smiles at her as her vision gets blurry with the pain. They come out of the room.

INT. CORRIDOR - NIGHT

Oscar continues to carry her through a corridor. Everything a blur. The pain. So intense. Moaning and crying.

A door.

INT. STAIRCASE - CONTINUOUS

Going down the stairs. Indistinct Chatter. Cursing.

INT. BASEMENT CORRIDOR - CONTINUOUS

More of the same. It feels like a nightmare. Nothing makes sense. Another door.

INT. BLACK ROOM - CONTINUOUS

Oscar DROPS her on the floor. GAGS her. TIES her to a CHAIR with tape.

She doesn't resist. Things still blurry until--

A BUCKET of COLD WATER SPLASHED ON HER.

Awake from the nightmare, only to discover it's real.

In front of her, Victor stands with a smile and a pair of PLIERS.

> VICTOR
> Hey. How are you?

> SASHA
> I--

He SMACKS her in the face with the PLIERS.

Her head turns and spins. Lin stands in front of her, tied up and gagged too. Her eyes very much alive.

> VICTOR
> As you can see, your friend is in
> good shape. Much better than now
> than in a few minutes. Glad you
> came back for the show, I was
> starting to worry you might miss
> it.

Oscar stands behind, perfectly still.

>   VICTOR (CONT'D)
>   Explain something to me. You could
>   have walked free. We'd lost track
>   of you. Completely.

He SMACKS her other cheek with the pliers.

>   VICTOR (CONT'D)
>   You came back for this terrible
>   excuse for a human being? Or is it
>   something else, such as Dmitri
>   sending you to me for completely
>   different reasons than what he told
>   me?

Sasha takes a deep breath. Ready to speak. Victor waits for a
smile.

>   SASHA
>   I come back to cut you in pieces.

Victor smiles.

>   VICTOR
>   I guess you failed. But you'll
>   still get to enjoy a similar
>   spectacle.

He gives the pair of PLIERS to Oscar, who grabs it.

Oscar crouches next to Lin. Avoids eye contact. Takes a deep
breath as Sasha watches him with pure fear. Lin begins to
WHIMPER.

CRUNCH. Lin SCREAMS like she never thought she could.

>   VICTOR (CONT'D)
>   How you like that? Nine more to go.
>   Then we get creative. Come on.

CRUNCH. More SCREAMING. Sasha looks enraged.

>   SASHA
>   What do you want?

Victor doesn't respond. Instead he nods to Oscar.

CRUNCH. More of the same.

>   SASHA (CONT'D)
>   Why are you doing this?

                         VICTOR
               I'm sorry honey. I just have to do
               this.

He nods. One more CRUNCH and all that comes with it. Oscar
grimaces briefly. Sasha catches it.

Sasha just watches in horror.

                         VICTOR (CONT'D)
               Let's stop for a moment.

He approaches Sasha. Grabs her jaw.

                         VICTOR (CONT'D)
               Tell me. What did Dmitri send you
               for?

She looks straight into his eyes.

                         SASHA
               To sell me to small dick pussy.

                         VICTOR
               Really?

Victor nods to Oscar. CRUNCH. SCREAM.

                         VICTOR (CONT'D)
               You think you're some sort of hero?

                         SASHA
               No.

                         VICTOR
               You're a little parasite.

He nods to Oscar. CRUNCH.

                         VICTOR (CONT'D)
               Everyone who gets close to you in
               any way just gets killed. Elena,
               Lin, your sister. They would all be
               fine without you.

That's too much for Sasha to hear. She YELLS and SQUIRMS in
her chair. This is the real torture.

                         VICTOR (CONT'D)
               And if you're not going to tell me
               the truth, I'll just enjoy watching
               you suffer.

Sasha looks down. Tears pouring down.

>   VICTOR (CONT'D)
>   But if you talk to me, I'll at
>   least spare Lin.

She looks up at her.

Her breathing like she just ran a marathon.

Stares at Victor.

>   SASHA
>   (under her breath)
>   I tell you truth.

Finally, she lets the tear come. Resigned.

>   SASHA (CONT'D)
>   He kill Daria. You right. I bad
>   news for everyone.

Victor, looking bored. Makes a sign to Oscar to keep going.

>   OSCAR
>   You do it.

>   VICTOR
>   What do you mean?

>   OSCAR
>   I will not.

>   VICTOR
>   What the fuck is this? You do what
>   I fucking tell you to do.

>   OSCAR
>   No.

He gets up and defies Victor with his look.

Victor doesn't smile. He pulls out his own gun, points it at
Lin. Holds it for a second. Cocks it.

Then quickly turns it to Oscar, who immediately grabs it.

Victor SHOOTS Oscar, but Oscar continues to STRUGGLE with
Victor, he's a tough motherfucker.

This is her chance.

In an ultimate effort, she GETS UP with her CHAIR attached to
herself, RUNS backwards to BREAK it as much as possible.

As the two men continue to BRAWL, she repeats the process.
SLAM! SLAM!

Oscar PUNCHES Victor to the ground.

Victor grabs his gun and finally SHOOTS Oscar in the chest.

Oscar drops on top of Victor, who STRUGGLES to push him away.

As soon as he does, Sasha DROPS herself (with the BROKEN
CHAIR) onto him.

Two BROKEN LEGS SLASH into Victor, one in his SHOULDER, the
other in his CROTCH.

He SCREAMS his lungs out.

She then pushes herself up. He screams some more.

It's over.

She turns to Lin.

                    SASHA
          Let me get us out of here.

She lets herself drop to the floor, then wiggles herself free
of the now almost destroyed chair.

Now free, she uses she still sharp broken chair leg to cut
through her ties.

Finally, she's free.

She runs to Lin and ungags her.

                    SASHA (CONT'D)
          Are you okay?

Lin whimpers madly, but makes an effort.

                    LIN
          Yes.

                    SASHA
          Where is the key?

                    LIN
          Oscar.

Sasha runs to Oscar, looks through his clothes and finds the
key.

She unshackles Lin.

The two embrace, SOBBING like didn't know they could.

Finally, Sasha breaks free.

>   SASHA
>   The others. And we need to leave.

INT. BASEMENT CORRIDOR - NIGHT

Sasha helps Lin walk with her limp. She now has something tied around her bleeding foot.

They try to open one of the basement doors, like one that used to lock them in. Locked. They pull as hard as they can. Nothing.

>   SASHA
>   We need key.

>   LIN
>   Where we find it?

Sasha thinks for a bit.

>   SASHA
>   Pete.

Lin understands. They need to go upstairs.

INT. 1ST FLOOR CORRIDOR - NIGHT

Sasha and Lin emerge from the staircase and head toward the security room when suddenly, they hear a SIREN coming from outside.

The cops.

They look at each other.

>   SASHA
>   Go get keys. I deal with them.

Lin nods.

Sasha heads for the front lobby, Lin heads for the back.

As she approaches the lobby, the BLUE and LIGHT reflections grow more saturated on the walls.

Everything is still dark, power hasn't been restored.

She reaches the lobby. Limping.

A COP CAR is parked across the front door, but no sign of cop until--

                    DUSTIN (O.S.)
          Freeze.

She turns to the side and sees Dustin, the cop she escaped from, facing her, shining his flashlight into her face, his gun pointed at her.

She raises her arms instinctively.

A closer look at him reveals part of his face is BURNT.

                    DUSTIN (CONT'D)
          I never thought I'd see you again.

He takes a step forward.

                    DUSTIN (CONT'D)
          I should kill you right now. But
          old Victor probably wants to do it
          himself.

He nods.

                    DUSTIN (CONT'D)
          Drop your gun, turn around, and
          take me to him.

She nods.

INT. CORRIDOR - NIGHT

Sasha leads him slowly, in silence. Every footstep heavier than the last. *She might die after all.*

They pass the staircase. *It's not over yet.*

She ends up leading him to the security room. They stop in front of the door.

                    DUSTIN
          Victor? You in there?

No response.

                    DUSTIN (CONT'D)
          What the fuck, you trying to fuck
          me, little bitch?

                    SASHA
          Never.

                              DUSTIN
                    Open the door.

He PUSHES her forward.

She opens the door and comes face to face with Lin, who is
now also holding a GUN she stole from one of the guards.

Sasha REACHES for Dustin's gun, trying to deflect it. He
SHOOTS into the wall. Twice.

                              SASHA
                    Lin!

Lin freezes. She can't do it.

Dustin SMACKS Sasha in the face with his free hand.

This motivates Lin. She SHOOTS before he can bring his gun
back to her.

Twice. Three times. The whole magazine. In Dustin's chest.

Lin breathing crazy fast.

Sasha looks at her in shock.

She walks to Lin. Grabs her shaky arms, then hugs her.
They're truly family now. Lin just saved her.

Lin still not realizing she just killed a man. Total shock.

Sasha and Lin stare at each other, breathing heavily. *They're
like sisters now.* They embrace again.

                         RAMIREZ (O.S.)
                    Freeze!

Stumbling, Sasha turns around and finds herself lit by a
FLASHLIGHT, held by OFFICER RAMIREZ (51), a tired cop who
actually understands the difference between justice and the
law.

She instinctively raises her hands.

                         RAMIREZ (CONT'D)
                    Drop your weapon!

Sasha looks to the side at Lin, who looks at her. Sasha nods.
Lin begins to cry again. *They were so close.*

Suddenly, a flurry of COPS run to them from behind Ramirez
and surround them.

Two of them handcuff Sasha and Lin one after the other, and push them on their knees.

The commotion around them becomes a blur.

EXT. THE FAIR FIELD - NIGHT

Several POLICE CARS are now parked out front, their red and blue LIGHTS DANCING against the WALLS.

A COUPLE AMBULANCE TRUCKS are there as well, their LIGHTS SHINING.

PARAMEDICS carry the dead bodies of Oscar and Dustin and treat the now free GIRLS in various places.

Officer Ramirez LEADS Sasha and Lin, toward his POLICE CAR.

Victor WHIMPERS from his own GURNEY when two GIRLS JUMP ONTO him and try to STRANGLE him.

Two officers immediately PULL them back, Victor COUGHS UP BLOOD from the assault, he looks more dead than alive now.

Sasha STRUGGLES to walk, she looks drowsy and in pain, but nobody seems to notice.

Lin looks around, then looks at Sasha.

                    LIN
           Sasha are you okay?

Sasha suddenly DROPS to the ground, unconscious.

                                  FADE TO:

INT. HOSPITAL ROOM - DAY

Sasha WAKES UP in a hospital bed, with bandages all over her body and face.

When she tries to HOIST herself up, she realizes her hand is HANDCUFFED to the bed.

She looks around the hospital room, a little helpless.

                    SASHA
           Hello?

She STRUGGLES with her handcuff. Nothing happens.

                         SASHA (CONT'D)
                    Anyone there?

The door opens at that moment. Detective Ramirez walks in
with a smile, followed by a POLICE OFFICER.

                         RAMIREZ
                    Hello there, how you doing?

                         SASHA
                    I could be better.

Ramirez chuckles.

                         RAMIREZ
                    Yeah, I can imagine.

He pauses, unsure how to proceed.

                         RAMIREZ (CONT'D)
                    I've done my preliminary
                    investigation.

                         SASHA
                    Am I in trouble?

                         RAMIREZ
                    Look, you should have gone to us.
                    You broke a lot of laws doing what
                    you did. But, you had a reasonable
                    cause not come to us. I'd like to
                    apologize about Officer Wayne, we
                    had no idea he was dirty.

Sasha looks at him, unsure what to think.

                         RAMIREZ (CONT'D)
                    With all things considered, it
                    could have gone a lot worse, and we
                    probably wouldn't have found out
                    what was going on there without
                    you.

He gives a sign to the officer, who leans in to unlock her
handcuff.

                         SASHA
                    Really? But--

                         RAMIREZ
                    Look, let's just say some of the
                    events that occurred at the Inn are
                    a little blurry, but as far as I'm
                    concerned, you and Lin are victims.

Sasha looks at him in disbelief. She feels her wrist in
relief.

                    SASHA
          What about Victor?

                    RAMIREZ
          He didn't make it, unfortunately.

He doesn't look too upset about it, neither does Sasha.

Lin enters the room, RUNS as fast as her feet allow her to
Sasha, and gives her a HUG. Sasha tries to hide the pain with
a smile.

                    LIN
          Sasha!

                    RAMIREZ
          I will let you two have a moment,
          one last thing. I understand you
          two might not want to ever set foot
          in this country again. But, there's
          a good chance you can get a green
          card after what happened to you
          both.

Lin and Sasha look at each other, barely able to understand.

                    RAMIREZ (CONT'D)
          Here's my card, contact me if you
          have any questions. I'll see you
          girls around.

He and the police officer leave the room.

Lin grabs Sasha's hand.

                    LIN
          How are you feeling?

Sasha smiles.

                    SASHA
          Good. You?

                    LIN
          My foot hurt. But I getting better.

                    SASHA
          Good.

Lin hesitates.

                    LIN
          Sasha?

                    SASHA
          Yes?

                    LIN
          What you going to do now? Go back?

Sasha smiles.

                    SASHA
          What are we going to do.

                    LIN
          You mean, you stay here-- with--
          me?

                    SASHA
          If we can.

Lin looks at Sasha in disbelief.

                    LIN
          So-- you not go back?

                    SASHA
          Let's get you to school first.

                    LIN
          We can get cat?

                    SASHA
          Yes, we can get cat.

Lin tears up and gives Sasha another heartfelt hug, which
Sasha begins to return.

                                        FADE OUT.

Manufactured by Amazon.ca
Bolton, ON

33861606R00059